IT'S YOUR TURN NOW!

******

Turning the Stumbling Blocks of your Past Into Stepping Stones for Your Future!

Debra D. Peppers, PhD

with

Susan DiChristina

It's Your Turn Now!, by Debra D. Peppers, Ph.D.
ISBN # 0-89228-088-3

Copyright © 2001 by Debra D. Peppers, Ph.D.

Published by
Impact Christian Books, Inc.
332 Leffingwell Ave.,
Kirkwood, MO 63122
314-822-3309

Cover Design: *Ideations*

All Scripture references are taken from the *New King James Version.,* unless otherwise specified.

CONTENTS

****

*****extension ideas*****

Acknowledgements

I believe that within each of us is a book waiting to be written. Mine has been "in the making" for forty-plus years! The chapters of our lives have been impacted by so many special people. It would be impossible to personally thank all of those who have "left their mark" on me and blessed me with their love and friendship; but as you read this book, you will hopefully realize my infinite gratitude!

Mom and Dad —- *Thank you for the gift of unconditional love, and for never giving up on me — even when I gave up on myself!*

My husband, Bud — *You never asked for anything but trust, something I had never known. You are my soul–mate, and the love of my life.*

Miss Alma — *Thank you for the gift of encouragement and for being the role–model for my teaching career.*

Suzy — *my former student, my editor, travel partner, co–writer, co–-conspirator, my friend who loves me in spite of the many faults you know so well — I owe you so much!*

My Family — *Thank you for loving me when I was so un-lovable, for encouraging me through my lost years, and for still being my best friends as well as my dear family.*

My Friends — *Though there are far too many names to list without leaving someone out, I hope you know how richly you have impacted my life. Thank you for always being there!*

My Colleagues — *Thank you for looking beyond my faults and idiosyncrasies, and encouraging me to go the next level by sharing your God–given strengths and talents that I so lack!*

My Former Students — *Thank you for letting me practice all my new life skills on you as I learned them. I hope I was a "Miss Alma" to you!*

My Prayer Partners, Church family, and Pastor and Faith Cutshall — *Only God knows how much I have needed your godly wisdom and appreciated your blanket of prayer! Please don't ever stop!*

****

Let us not be weary in well doing: for in due season we shall reap, if we faint not.   Galatians 6:9

Foreword

My Darling Baby Girl,

     I write this as you have threatened to run away again and I am leaving this on your pillow with the hopes that you will get it before you leave. I know at 17 you are a young woman now and we can't stop you from going. Your Mom and I have asked ourselves a thousand times where we went wrong…where we failed you. I would give anything if we could go back to the days when you were Daddy's little girl and would snuggle up on my lap and bring all your hurts and wounds to me to "make better." I only blame myself for all that has gone wrong and would give my very life for another chance to make it right. I didn't see soon enough how much you were hurting. Mommy and I have prayed and cried for you more than you will ever know and have asked if we were too strict or too lenient, too giving or not giving enough. All we know is that we love you and want you to talk to us. Please reconsider before you leave again and let's see if we can't work it out one more time. Dearest Debbie Girl, we love you with no strings attached. God brought you to us and no matter what, you will always be our precious baby girl. When you come home and read this, no matter how late it is, please come talk to us. We love you so much!

Always,
Your Loving Daddy

I didn't get to read Dad's letter that night as I had already run away from home and wouldn't return for six weeks. The road beyond that night was even rockier still. I would drop out of high school, experiment with drugs and alcohol, even try to take my own life. But Mom and Dad saved that letter and presented it to me for the first time some twenty years later, the night of the Missouri State Teacher of the Year Banquet in the Rotunda of the Missouri State Capitol. I was one of the top five teachers in the state, being honored along with our families and school administrators. I thought I was opening a little gift box from my parents containing a pendant or medal inscribed with "Teacher of the Year." Instead, I received this letter and wept like a baby. Neither my parents nor I could have ever imagined in our wildest dreams that my life would have turned around so radically from those "lost" years. I thank God that my parents were finally able to see the fruits of their labor. All their past struggles, all the sleepless nights, and the worrying had finally been worth it all. I am living proof that re-making your life is possible, for those who think it's too late or even for those who consider themselves failures. The formula is not special, exclusive, or even top–secret! If I can do it, I promise you that anyone can!

Prologue

As painful as it is at times for my family and me to re–visit the old haunting memories of a time we would easily like to forget, we all agree on one thing. If sharing our troubled past helps just one soul on the face of the earth, then it is well worth it. I will never be able to thank my Mom and Dad, my husband and family for the love they always gave beyond measure. The most valuable lesson they taught to me (me, the teacher), was to also love unconditionally, even the most unlovable of all. They genuinely modeled for me the infinite love of Jesus Christ Himself, even before I knew Him or how much He loved me. For that I will be eternally grateful.

I don't presume to know your life's story, the ups and downs, or the successes and failures you may have experienced. However, having taught ten-thousand high school and college students through the years and having traveled in all fifty states and over fifty foreign countries, I know one thing for sure: I have yet to meet one person whose life has unfolded exactly as they imagined it would. In fact, I believe that everyone has a story to tell – a book inside of them that is waiting to be written. And for most of us it always includes a multitude of unexpected twists and turns.

Sometimes we have no choice when life takes us down a different path than we originally intended through no fault of our own. We may be forced to change course due to an accident, illness, or tragedy. For some of us, we may have been our own worst enemies. We may have at times created our own obstacles to success and happiness. Other times, life's potential has passed us by because we didn't seize the opportunities that presented themselves. Or perhaps we just left things to chance, and thought, "Whatever!"

Then one day we wake up and find ourselves in a different place from where we wanted to be. The one thing that we thought we would have achieved by now seems so elusive. Perhaps we have lost the passion that once drove us, or maybe we just decided life is too hard.

My friend, you may have even given up on your once vibrant dreams. You might be convinced that you can't become or achieve what you once imagined – those dreams you had as a child, when the world was an open book and the possibilities were infinite. You might simply believe that it's just too late for you.

Thousands of highly successful people began pursuing their "lost" dream under extremely adverse conditions, whether it was due to circumstances beyond their control or the self-inflicted wounds of poor choices. At some point along the way, they stopped in the middle of what seemed to be the inevitable wrong direction – they somehow changed their course, and became one of those "before and after" success stories. What made the difference? What kept them from falling through the cracks like thousands of others in similar situations? What made them go back and pick up those old, lost dreams and begin once again to pursue them passionately? How did they go from living in a state of chronic negativity, or constant chaos, or destined failure, to truly living out the dream they originally sought?

My purpose for writing this book is to share my story – and in so doing to give the gift of encouragement for others to change their lives as well! Every audience, practically every place I speak wants me to tell my "before and after" story and how I was able make that change. They want to know how I lost 100 pounds, how my parents dealt with such a juvenile delinquent, and how I could have gone so wrong coming from such a good family. But more than anything, they want to know what I did initially to make change happen, then how long it took, and how they too can walk away with hope for change – whether it's for their child, or their friend, or loved one, or for themselves.

I will share with you famous folks who were told they "couldn't," but did, as well as the ugly truth of my own personal story. But I will also share with you the motivation strategies and practical steps that others and I have found successful, that will also help to get you on track and back to pursuing your dreams. You will see the importance of determination, how to overcome obstacles and actually make them work for you, as well as how to live a balanced life as you keep moving to higher levels. As you assess what is truly important in your life, you may even learn a few things about yourself that you never knew. But three important truths I promise you.

God has a perfect plan for your life and it's never too late to find it! Whatever your past or present obstacles are, you can write your own success story. The balanced, successful life you dreamed of can come true! So if you are truly ready, if you want to change or you know someone who is, then congratulations! You are well on the way. Get ready for the best of your life!

If I can do it, anyone can!

One

BEFORE AND AFTER

If anyone is in Christ, he is a new creation; the old has gone and the new has come!
                                                                –2:Corinthians 5:17

Thomas Edison, *America's greatest inventor*, was labeled as "too stupid to learn" by his teachers.

Lucille Ball, *Actress and Comedienne*, failed her first drama class. Her acting teacher told her that she "had no talent."

William Faulkner, *Winner of the 1949 Nobel Prize in Literature*, earned a "D" in English and was rejected as a member of the Ole Miss Literary Society.

Michael Jordan, *6-time NBA Champion*, was cut from his high school basketball team his junior year.

Albert Einstein, *Nobel Prize winning physicist*, did not talk until age 4 and didn't read until 9. He failed math, his college entrance exam, and was judged to have "no promise."

Abraham Lincoln, *16th President of the United States*, was defeated in his first election to the Illinois State legislature, lost in a bid to Congress, and was twice defeated in election to the U.S. Senate.

Eleanor Roosevelt, *First Lady, Humanitarian, Diplomat*, was plagued by shyness as a child and fainted the first time she tried to speak in public.

Walt Disney, *Film Animator, Producer*, was fired by a newspaper editor because he had "no good ideas."

Isaac Newton, *Physicist and Mathematician*, did poorly in grade school and flunked mathematics.

Mahatma Gandhi, *Political Activist, Philosopher,* was a below average student and failed every subject during his first attempt at college, withdrawing after only five months.

Jackie Joyner-Kersee, *World–Class Track and Field Athlete*, has suffered from asthma her entire life.

Dr. Debra Peppers, *Inducted into the National Teachers Hall of Fame,* was a high school dropout and troubled teen.r.
****

I am certainly not rich or famous as are those listed above me, but I have one thing in common: I am one of life's overcomers. I don't say this in boasting: you will see, I take very little credit for my success. I thank God for the strategic people He placed in my life when I needed them most, and I thank Him for life's lessons. These are the strategies I will share with you throughout this book as so many others have shared with me.

As I have taught thousands of high school and college students, and presented to hundreds of audiences through the years, I have had the great fortune of interacting with people from all over the world and from all walks of life. I talk with people I meet, and others I only know through my radio or television program. One common thread that everyone shares is that all have a unique life story. People are often eager to reveal their triumphs and fears, successes and failures, and their hopes and dreams. They often identify with my life's story. I'm not at all proud that I have had my share of pain and regret; but I thank God for the radical, life-altering change that brings joy, fulfillment, and deep personal reward. If there is one lesson that my life story can teach, it is that God is still in the miracle business and I'm living proof!

I share my story with you as a witness to what's possible – that failure does not have to be permanent and that the abundant life is well within your reach. Despite what you may have been told or what you believe, you have all the skill and talent you need to live a rewarding life you may have only dreamed until now. You don't have to be famous, wealthy, well–born, brilliant, or even beautiful. I was never any of these things. In fact, I've learned that God's most extraordinary miracles happen to ordinary people – people like you and me.

My story begins in the small town of Clarksville, Missouri, just north of St. Louis, on the banks of the mighty Mississippi. Route 79, the "Great River Road," winds through the center of town, linking Clarksville to other picturesque hamlets in the Midwest. Like hundreds of small towns that dot America's heartland, Clarksville was wholesome, quaint, neighborly, and secure. The population has hovered around 500 residents, give or take a few, for as long as I can remember. Growing up there during the 1950's and 1960's was as close to the "Beaver Cleaver" idyll as you could get. No one locked their doors or worried about drugs or crime. Most people born in Pike County, Missouri settled there, invested in the schools, churches, and the community. Everyone knew everyone and life was pleasantly simple.

As an adolescent, I somehow became an exception to the norn of the day, utterly lost, in ways that too many kids are today. As I grew up, I began turning to food for comfort, and I became extremely overweight and withdrawn from my friends. Since I never felt good about myself, I compensated by acting out in harmful ways. If anyone had told my high school teachers that one day I too would become a teacher, half of them would have laughed in disbelief, and the other half would have cried. I was a well–known troublemaker. I had been in and out of the principal's office and suspended so many times my family had become the talk of the town.

My sister, Donna, was my idol and my role model. She was four years older and had always been everything I wanted to be: Head Cheerleader, Prom Queen Valedictorian, Yearbook Queen, and the model student every parent wants. My younger brother Duke was just as successful: star athlete, student council, A+ student, popular, good looking and charismatic. Then, there was "Poor Debbie." I heard that name applied to me so often that I lost count. In my small town, I was a well-known trouble-maker, runaway, and on the verge of dropping out of Clopton High School. No wonder everyone spoke of my family and their "poor middle child." I wasn't necessarily doomed to failure for I grew up in a loving, traditional family. My mom and dad were hard working, middle class parents who did all that they could to provide a good home for their children. From my earliest memory, I never doubted how much my parents loved my siblings and me. They were devoted parents, actively involved in their children's upbringing. They had been to school numerous times on my behalf. They took me to counselors and doctors and were always trying to rescue me from my abyss. Every time I got into trouble, or ran away from home, or needed to be re-instated in school, or bailed out of jail, or caught cheating or fighting, my parents were always there for me. They had tried everything and they were left frustrated and helpless.

Like all kids growing up, I had dreams of the person I wanted to be. I remember once pretending to be a preacher, and then a radio announcer, and sometimes a famous actress. I wish I could put my finger on the age where I started to rebel and "go wrong." According to my parents, I had been a beautiful baby and happy toddler. When I look at photos and growth charts of me at five years old, I was average in height, but alerady overweight. I first remember being called "Fatty" by a boy I had a crush on in the 3rd grade. My teacher, Mrs. Buchanan, reprimanded him; but it was at that moment, age 8, that I experienced my first humiliation. It would be only the first of hundreds of humiliating experiences.

Over the next few years, I went from being a loving, confident, good student following in my sister's footsteps, to the "poor fat kid" that everybody picked on. How loving parents can raise two girls four years apart and have them turn out as polar opposites puzzles me. Donna loved to study and was somewhat of a perfectionist. I always managed to squeak by at the last minute, never studying for tests, often writing papers on the bus, or copying when I got to school. I lost all semblance of a conscience by Junior High and had become so angry at being called names and teased, so frustrated at not being able to lose weight, and so envious of my closest friends, I began to do anything that would gain attention. Looking back, I was crying out for help, but in all the wrong ways.

I turned more and more to food for comfort. I watched my friends growing into beautiful, young ladies, going to school dances and on dates. I hid in my room with a half–gallon of ice cream and I began to take all my frustration out on my poor parents who had already begun to seek professional help for me.

As my volatile teen years progressed, I grew increasingly hostile and indifferent, playing the "victim" role. I began to intimidate my classmates and believed that many of them were afraid of me. My parents were afraid *for* me, and fearful of what I might become. The more my mom tried to help me diet and bought me exercise equipment, the more I resented how beautiful and slim she and Donna were. They were both beautiful. My dad and younger brother were "buddies" as Dad coached the little league where my brother was the star pitcher. I always felt alienated and sensed that I was an embarrassment to my family, my school, the whole town.

Like so many kids today, I felt that my life had no purpose. I was confused, angry, and depressed. At 250 lb. and hating everyone and everything, I wanted to hide all the time. I didn't want to go to school, but I didn't want to stay home either. When my grades and self–worth continued to plummet, I gave up trying. It was much easier to get attention by being the "class clown." I no longer believed that I could measure up to what people expected. When I convinced myself that I couldn't be the child that my parents wanted me to be, it was so easy to be the opposite – and that's exactly what I did.

Thirty years ago I set the standard for a parent's worst nightmare. I dyed my hair orange by using straight Clorox bleach. It wasn't long before my hair began to fall out in big patches. I also fashioned the most atrocious wardrobe I could dream up to hide my obesity, while I unknowingly drew more negative attention to myself. I pierced my own ears with a needle. I began smoking and drinking to be cool. I tried to make friends with a few older kids from the "wrong side of the tracks" and the worse I became, the better my delinquent friends liked me. I was relieved to be accepted for doing what came so naturally – being a bad kid. If there had been access to drugs and gangs in Clarksville back then, I would have been an easy target, perhaps even a ringleader recruiting all the other misfits and troubled teens. I wasn't just an "Eddie Haskell" to my perfect "Cleaver" family. I was an outcast, a failure, and a pariah – at least in my own eyes. And back then, that's all that really mattered.

The last time I ran away from home, my parents could not locate me for weeks as I stayed any place I could find. I soon discovered that "freedom" didn't solve my problems. Soon with nowhere to live, no job, and no money, I found life outside my safe haven could be hard, cruel, and even dangerous. Like a prodigal child, I returned home to my family who always welcomed me back with open arms. But this time, they set the much-needed boundaries. I could only return home, if I agreed to live by their rules. I reluctantly returned to school.

The first day back was as miserable as I had anticipated. I heard all the names as my peers jeered, "Hey Fatso!" or "The jailbird is back!" I probably would have run away again had it not been for the familiar voice from the end of the hall. Mrs. Alma Sitton, who let us fondly call her "Miss Alma," had been one teacher who had always treated me with respect and dignity. However, she was tough on all of us and immersed us in literature, speech, and grammar. We all knew if we missed one day of Miss Alma's class, she had the neat stacks of make-up work ready for us! This time I had been absent for weeks!

Ignoring the taunts of my classmates, I dutifully trudged down the hall as Miss Alma called to me. As expected, she ushered me into her warm, familiar classroom, near the table of missed assignments. I said nothing as I rolled my eyes, bit my tongue, and waited for a lecture to accompany the piles of missed homework. Miss Alma quietly closed the door. What came next was so totally unexpected! Miss Alma turned toward me with her back to the table and did the most paradoxical, most unbelievable thing that any teacher had ever done! She put her purple, "ditto-streaked" hands on my shoulders, looked me straight in the eyes down to my soul, and then put her arms around me! As she hugged me tightly, Miss Alma whispered softly in my ear, "Debbie, God has great plans for your life, if you'll let Him. And I'm here for you, too." I vaguely remember the piles of homework she began explaining, but I will never forget the gift of hope and encouragement she gave me that day. That ten–second gift has lasted thirty years. I may not remember all the assignments that day, but Miss Alma became my hero. I enrolled in all the classes that Miss Alma taught. I wanted to be around her, because she believed in me. More than that, she helped me believe in God - and myself. Although my encounter with Miss Alma that day did not permanently "fix" my problems, it did help me make it through high school. I also know it wasn't a coincidence that I would become an English, speech, and drama teacher – just like Miss Alma.

Regrettably, as I moved on after high school, I returned to my old habits and the same destructive path. But that day in her classroom, Miss Alma had planted seeds of hope and faith that would eventually take root and grow. Those of you who feel like giving up on the "prodigals" in your life, keep praying and stay strong!

I could write chapters about my horrible college years, but I will spare you the sordid details. From trying prescription amphetamines for weight loss and depression to being on academic probation, to attempting suicide more than once, I was on a one–way, self–destructive path. Then once again God intervened and sent me an angel. "Bud"

Peppers from Mobile, Alabama was too good to be true. He was the first man of honesty and integrity I had ever loved — other than my own father. I had actually become so cynical and suspicious of men that I was sure he wasn't real. Thirty years later, he is still the love of my life, my best friend and my God–send.

But just as my loving family, the ideal hometown, and an inspiring teacher had not been enough to change my life — even the man that would become my husband and life–long companion, couldn't solve my problems and give me that elusive "happiness." Through more heartaches, fruitless job searches, psychologists, pursuit of dangerous religious cults, more drinking, smoking, and drugs, and, of course, more weight gain, I finally had one last bout with attempted suicide. But this time, I saw in the mirror the culmination of all I had become and the manifestation of evil personified. I finally cried out for the one source I hadn't tried. After 23 years of searching in every wrong place, I finally cried out to God for help. My parents, Sunday school teachers, Miss Alma, my college roommate and now my husband had all told me and shown me God's love. Now I encountered it for myself. He has promised me not only eternal life, but life abundantly right here, right now. That was over twenty–five years ago and life is more wonderful, more joyful, and more exciting every year. That same promise is for YOU!

If you are ready to step out in faith and take the steps needed to have and live that overcoming life, then put on your seat belt and get ready for the ride of your life! The best is yet to come. But first, we must take a look backward in order to move forward. Just take a quick glance in your rearview mirror to make sure the enemy isn't gaining territory. And no matter how far you go from here on, and no matter how successful you become, the first important rule is this: *NEVER FORGET WHERE YOU HAVE BEEN, SO YOU CAN HELP OTHERS ON THE WAY TO WHERE THEY'RE GOING!*

There's another great saying that "Every time you lead others to the mountaintop, you get to re–visit it yourself." You will find that the real success you cherish most is not in the success of what you achieve, but in how many others you help along the way. NOW IT'S YOUR TURN. Here is your first assignment:

IN A PARAGRAPH OR MORE, WRITE YOUR SIGNA-TURE STORY, YOUR TESTIMONY, OR WHATEVER YOU WANT TO CALL IT. Your past is the first part of your story – good, bad, or ugly …but it's not the end! You may, or may not, have had much of a choice in it – at least your story up to this point. But this is where to begin. What happens next? The rest of the story is just enfolding. It's up to you!

MY STORY

_____

_____

_____

_____

_____

_____

Two

SO WHAT DO YOU WANT TO DO WITH THE REST OF YOUR LIFE?

The thief comes only to steal, kill and destroy; I came that they may have life and have it abundantly.
—John 10:10 (RSV)

In traveling around the world the past few years, my husband and I have been absolutely amazed, inspired, intrigued, and mesmerized by the unsung heroes we have met. There are so many people who, in spite of past circumstances, are truly living out their dreams! What is most astonishing is that many of them didn't get on the right track, so to speak, until they were in their fifties, sixties, seventies, or beyond!

We met a precious Chinese great-grandmother in her eighties who was hiking down from "The Great Wall." Growing up a poor servant girl in Beijing, she had raised her own family while sewing for a wealthy family. She was determined to open her own shop, which she later did. Her business earned enough money to travel to the places she had once only dreamed of visiting.

One dear African–American gentleman from Texas didn't learn to read until he was 97 years old! George heard that a local community group was offering to teach literacy to senior citizens. He simply asked, "Why not?" Not only did he learn how to read, but at age 101 he published his first book *Life is Beautiful*. Many folks told him he was too old; but he would have been just as old whether he learned to read or not.

A friend of mine, Elizabeth, decided when her children were grown and through college, that it was her turn. She had saved enough for her first semester's tuition and proudly announced to her family that she was going to go back to school and pursue a degree in English. One of her grown children said, "Mom, you are fifty-one years old! You will be 55 by the time you graduate!" She simply queried, "And how old will I be in four years if I *don't* go back to school?" Liz, now a very successful editor and free–lance writer, is still going strong at age 64!

Most of us get so busy and so caught up in the day to day routine – the "gerbil treadmill" of life, as I like to refer to it – that we not only don't stop long enough to really appreciate life, the treadmill *becomes* our life – and we don't know how to get off! The most demoralizing lie that the enemy whispers in our ear is "You can't do that!" We are too quick to think we are too old, too incompetent, too uneducated, not smart enough, and a thousand other lies that keep us from fulfilling the plan God has – and always has had – for each of our lives!

For I know the plans I have for you, declares the Lord, plans to prosper you and not to harm you, plans to give you hope and a future.
— Jeremiah 29:11 (NIV)

So before we go any further, you need to stop right now and take a small personal inventory. For just a moment, don't even think about what you *can't* do, but take a little trip with me back in time. The negative tape you may have been playing in your mind for who knows how long is be-

ing put into reverse. Go back five, ten, twenty, fifty years –
however long it takes you to get back to fourth or fifth grade.
Try to picture yourself then.

A recent study reported that the person you were at age
9 or 10 (your personality, your likes, your attitude, your
dreams) is pretty much what you should be like as an adult!
The study confirmed that the dreams we formulate during
our early years often accurately reflect our deepest desires
as adults. Obviously, some of you may have gone through
certain tragedies or catastrophes that alter this path or direction. Putting any diversions aside, how did you see yourself
back then? At age 9 or 10, what were your hobbies and
what did you want to be when you grew up? If you will
really be honest, you had *great* dreams, high ideals, and
expectations. In your naiveté and childlike innocence, you
thought you could conquer the world, be anything you
wanted to be! You knew you would marry the right person,
have the perfect family and live in the perfect house in the
perfect location and live happily ever after! As carefree
children our world was full of wonder, of new adventures
every day. We had new friends, new activities, and the whole
world was ours to conquer. We lived life spontaneously.
We would sing out loud and play in the rain and dance on
the steps and roll in grass and run barefoot in the mud and….

And somewhere we lost it!

Some of you may have had a traumatic childhood over
which you had no control. But the very place you have been
hurt the most is where God can use you to help others. But
you must first heal, get free and move on UP! What the
enemy meant for harm, God will use for good!

Each of us – somewhere, somehow – lost that wide-
eyed innocence and *joie de vivre* that most of us would give
anything to have back! It was a sense of *wonder!*

We start to rationalize by saying "If I only had…" like the Scarecrow, the Tin Man, and the Lion in the Wizard of Oz. "If I only had a brain" – "If I only had a heart" – "If I only had the nerve" etc. We use our shortcomings, or perceived inadequacies, as an excuse for why we didn't become the person we dreamed of becoming when we were young.

Well, I have great news for you! You **CAN** have it back. You can go back to your original dreams and hopes and the plans that God had for your life! It doesn't matter how old you are, or what your circumstances, there is **POWER** in hooking up with the King of the Universe and tapping into the source of HIS power! I don't care what voice you have been listening to, telling you that you can't, that you'll fail, you'll make a fool of yourself, or that you're no good. Stop that tape running in your head, playing that worn-out useless message over and over, and listen to what Scripture tells us. Jesus himself said that we are to come as a little child! And we ARE his children! We are to be childlike (not child-ISH) and learn to trust HIM! Even when all others may have let us down!

You can scream and cry and pout and sulk and say, "But I have tried everything to turn my life around – to move to a higher level of living – and I'm happy for those who have, but I can't do it! Maybe I was just destined to be a failure!" Some might just walk away from you and leave you to wallow in your pity. But I can't do that because I've been there. I was the queen of pity parties and I lived in that state of constant negativity for far too many years. I found THE way out, and THE way up, and IT'S YOUR TURN NOW! If you are really serious, this is all about living life on a higher plane, where even in the midst of every day trials and tribulations, illogical and irritating people, temptations

28

and struggles, you can still have peace, joy, hope, confidence, perseverance, and keep moving forward! Of course, there will always be occasional setbacks here and there. We can expect that! So what?

So now, we are ready to move on anyway! Get a pencil and be ready to take a good look deep inside as you pray that God will reveal to you honestly – and He is always honest – your shortcomings as well as your untapped gifts and waiting-to-be-used talents. You may have made New Year's Resolutions in the past; you may have tried a thousand self–help programs, gone on a zillion diets, or sought get rich quick schemes. The next chapter is all about YOU! You are not just going to look at the past and into your soul, but you are going to begin positive, proactive principles that you will practice from now on – life-changing, earth-shattering changes that will literally rock your world! No, I am not selling you a magic pill or potion. I am not advocating some religious program or guru to follow. All I know is what worked for me, for thousands of my former students, fellow colleagues, teachers, friends, senior citizens, and folks around the world for two thousand years! It is tried and true and never fails. I just wish someone had told me sooner — well, I suppose they did. But I had to be ready to listen, to take it in, and to live it out. If you are really ready, if you know there has to be more to life than this, then IT'S YOUR TURN NOW!

"If I Only Had a …"

Be honest about the "negative tape" you have been playing over and over in your mind. List the shortcomings or inadequacies you have told yourself that keep you from achieving your dreams. Whether they are real or perceived, list them!

Three

START YOUR ENGINES!

As a prisoner for the Lord, then, I urge you to live a life worthy of the calling you have received.
—*Ephesians 4:1 (NIV)*

Start by doing what is necessary, then do what is possible, and suddenly you are doing the impossible.
—*St. Francis of Assisi*

At the beginning of any race, everyone begins behind the starting line. This means that someone may already occupy the "pole position" – possessing an advantage, based on past experience, or performance, or learned technique. But it also doesn't mean there won't be an unforeseen problem or accident or trouble at the pit stop. There isn't any guarantee that anyone, including those at the pole position, will actually win or place or even finish the race. But there is one thing for sure:

IF YOU NEVER START YOUR ENGINE,
YOU'LL NEVER GO ANYWHERE!

As an English teacher, I would often begin class with a writing prompt, presenting a topic or showing a picture to illicit the students' impressions of the subject matter. I would give them ten minutes and remind them that they would receive credit for the initial journal entry. As this task was a brainstorming activity, the purpose was to get them in the habit of simply writing. I reminded them not to worry about the technical aspects; that we would later go back and correct the spelling, grammar, and write revisions. All I wanted them to do was to get their thoughts on paper and simply begin composing. The students received ten points just for filling the page. For most of them, it was an easy assignment and they looked forward to it – especially since I would bring in interesting objects from around the world, or give them a favorite teen topic such as music, cars, sports, or favorite food.

Inevitably, there were one or two students who would sit, staring silently at the paper for the entire ten minutes and never write a word! When I was a beginning teacher, I would take this lack of response personally. I would become either hurt or outraged to think they were just being belligerent or defiant. Later as I became more experienced, I might suspect that the student had a learning disability or perhaps didn't understand the instructions. But nine times out of ten I found there was only one real problem – **fear of failure**! When I finally built a trusting relationship with the students, they would confide in me as to why they wrote NOTHING. In their own way they would admit to me that they would rather receive no credit at all than to risk failing. Whether it happened to be a student who was afraid one of their peers might read what they wrote and make fun of them, or another who was afraid I would have them read it out loud and they would die of embarrassment, or even an occasional perfectionist who knew there was not enough time to write, re-write, and correct all mistakes, they each chose not to even begin the task!

We have all heard the adages about the importance of

taking one step at a time. The only way to eat an elephant is one bite at a time, and Rome wasn't built in a day. We KNOW all of that. So why is it that some people can begin and persevere and take life in increments, the good and the bad? They still fall down, but keep getting up. But there are still those who won't even try – *those who for whatever reason don't even begin!* Will Rogers is famous for saying, "Even if you're on the right track, you'll get run over, if you just sit there."

Some of you have tried everything there is to try – or so you say. And you may have tried something a hundred times and failed. I can't tell you how many diets and weight loss gimmicks and "I Promise You'll Lose Weight" schemes I tried through the years! But I didn't lose weight until I got to the end of my rope and to the end of myself and to the end of all the schemes and dreams and wishful thinking! Whatever your dream or desire or hope, whether it is to lose weight, improve your marriage, find the right job, go back to school, change your attitude, or just find joy in living each day, there are a couple of things you must agree to do:

1.   Learn from Past Mistakes

Look back honestly to learn from past mistakes. Don't dwell unproductively on all the old issues. And don't make this process some psychological babble game of getting in a fetal position and finding your inner lost child while chanting bird calls. This exercise is simply understanding and never forgetting your areas of weakness that may "trip you up" again, if you don't remain proactive and on the alert! Some battle past abuse, some drugs and alcohol, co-dependent relationships, promiscuity, overeating or food disorders, unwise spending or greed. This list could be infinite; but if we are honest, it won't take long to find our nemesis.

2. Examine Your God–given Talents

Take an unbiased look at your strengths and talents and past dreams. For some this is fairly easy. Those with honest esteem can be impartial about what they do well. Those who are insecure or self–loathing may think they have NO talents or gifts! And the arrogant may think they do everything better than anyone else. So above all else, be honest! If you choose, find a friend or relative who knows you well and have them share your strengths with you. Loved ones can help you with the first step as well – if you are brave enough. One lady approached me when I was speaking at a women's retreat and told me about a church Bible study she attended on "Finding Your Gift." She said she found out she had none! After asking her a few questions about her background, her loving relationships, and her childhood dreams, we discovered that she was a great organizer (the gift of administration). She also loved to be with children and admitted to being a great listener for friends who often came to her for advice (the gift of encouragement). As a child, she wanted to be a teacher, coach or counselor. We made a list of 30 ways she could use these talents today – from teaching Sunday school, to going back to school and getting a degree, to volunteering in the nursery or local school, coaching, or even donating her time to a crisis hotline. She did several!

3. Start With Small Steps

Be willing to BEGIN to take small, consistent steady steps to bring about needed change – or at least *be willing to be **made** willing*! For instance, if you really don't want to stop smoking and don't see any real health needs to do so, you probably won't quit. But if you are tired of wasting your money, having to go outside at your work place, you know you have nasty cough and smoker's breath, your family and friends complain or you hate it that a stupid little rolled up weed has control over your mind, your body, and perhaps even your spirit, then maybe you are ready to take the first step! My husband and I quit together over 20 years ago and, honestly, we just about got a divorce or killed each other! But someone told me that it takes only 21 days to break a habit. So I swam and exercised more and ate healthy and drank a lot of water. As our reward, every penny that would have been spent on cigarettes (4 packs a day between the two of us) was put into an investment toward an eventual swimming pool. Prayer was my mainstay and only God got us through those 21 days. We both knew how weak the flesh was and, if we had ever allowed ourselves to smoke "just one" back then, it would have been all over. This was probably the hundredth time we had tried to stop. But that time it worked. Now whenever I swim in my indoor, greenhouse swimming pool, I thank God that we "pooled" that money in a very wise investment!

4. Be Kind When You Stumble

Learn how to NOT beat yourself up when you stumble or fail. One of my favorite old gospel tunes pleads, "One Day at a Time, Sweet Jesus, is all I'm asking of You!" How many times have we started a new plan, a new resolution, or a new diet, only to "blow it" within the first hour! So then it's all or nothing. We allow ourselves guilt-free indulgence promising ourselves we will begin again tomorrow! *Remember that today is the tomorrow you promised yourself yesterday!* Don't let that worn out tape keep playing those same old lies in your head! If it has to be one hour at a time or even *one minute* at a time, begin again! When a baby falls every time he tries to walk, do we think, "What is the matter with that stupid baby? He will never learn to walk!" Or do we, conversely, pick the baby up every time and walk his little legs for him? No, of course not! Babies learn to walk by falling and getting up, falling and getting up, one little baby step at a time. We encourage, praise and patiently endure along with the baby. We all learned to walk this way at one time! Isn't the principle the same with life's other lessons? I am the queen of instant gratification and used to never wait in line, raced ahead of everyone on the highway, never denied myself food or pleasure- or anything! And at age 23 I almost died as a result. Patience is indeed a hard-learned virtue, but what peace and joy accompany it!

5. Be Confident, Not Prideful

There is a fine line between confidence and pride, and the latter cometh before a fall! Using the same baby analogy, we are delighted at the big toothless grin and self–applause of a baby who takes those first steps and remains standing. We applaud with him and tell him how big and smart and special he is. But when we call our friend whose baby is older and hasn't even stood alone yet, just to gloat over how much more advanced *our* baby is, that's pride. Most of us can think of a time when we truly did something outstanding, achieved an honor or award or some accolade from our peers. We may have truly worked hard and really deserved the applause. We should feel a degree of satisfaction. But this is where God looks at our heart, our motives, and what we do with that measure of success. If you have a dream or goal or desire for the future simply to store up treasures for yourself, or for fame, or to show old so-and-so that you got the better of him, then get ready for the proverbial fall! Scripture makes it perfectly clear that, "If someone thinks he is something, beware lest he fall." Jesus told the rich young ruler that he had to sell everything and give it to the poor in order to enter the Kingdom of Heaven! Why was this young rich man the only one in the Bible that Jesus told this? Because Jesus saw the pride in the young man's heart and the bragging on his lips, as he told Jesus he had done everything right and kept all the laws. But money was his first love and Jesus knew it. We cannot love both God and mammon (money). In other words, if there is something in your life that takes precedence over God or your fellow man, even something *good*, such as your accomplishments, they must be abased. I thank God every day that I have so many "before" pictures to remind me what I was like as a 250-pound angry, self-indulgent, 23-year old who wanted to die. I must never lose sight of all that I was on my *self–made* path of destruction, so I can *know* who I am in Christ and what He has allowed me to become by His grace, mercy, and love. His path and plan for my life was always there; I just had to get to the end of mine. Maybe your self–made path wasn't so destructive. Perhaps you are more like the rich young ruler, or the Pharisee who said, "Thank God I am not like the beggar in the street." Or maybe you truly love God and are humbly seeking His will for your life but just can't seem to find it! Keep seeking – God has planned the most fulfilling life for you and you will find it if you persist!

6. Use Setbacks as Bridges to Success

Life is full of twists and turns. Expect obstacles and setbacks, but learn to use them. Remember those 1000 piece jigsaw puzzles where there was always that one piece you couldn't find. You tried to match colors and shapes and even force in a piece that didn't fit? I left the wrong piece in one time, knowing it wasn't right, but it temporarily relieved my frustration, that is until it left an even worse mess! I soon had pieces and places with no matches! Thomas Edison once said, "I have not failed. I've just found 10,000 ways that don't work." Every failed puzzle piece gets you that much closer to finding the right place where it DOES fit. And when the picture starts to take shape, it's amazing how much easier finishing is, once you have established momentum. But think of all the people that give up and barely even begin their "life's puzzle" – much less finish!

7. Don't Be Afraid to Ask for Help

Be willing to ask for help, take off the martyr's mask, and be as kind to yourself as you would your best friend. And, be willing to forgive! This is a key ingredient! Down the road you will be blessed, as others will then come to *you* for help and advice. There was a time in my life when I was too proud and too self-sufficient to ask anything of anybody. And certainly no one wanted the life I had, so why would they come to me for help? I was angry, bitter, and hated the world – and myself! I was so self-deceived, I didn't even think others knew how pitiful I really was.

8. Choose to Be Joyful

Learn to live more in the present – to enjoy life on purpose! Begin to be an encourager to yourself as well as those around you. Even if you are the most negative, hateful, mean-spirited, self-centered person in the whole world (and by the way, you aren't!), be willing right now to take back those wonderful childlike traits you used to have and let go of what you have become. Find joy in each person, place, and experience you encounter each day. Laugh at yourself and begin to marvel at how you can *choose* to find good in the worst thing that happens– even when your human nature wants to cry out the most hateful obscenity! Even that emotion can be turned around. There is a way to overcome (not just get through it!).

9. Stand Naked Before God

Okay, maybe not literally. But as we bare our souls, and are humbled in our spirit before Him, we surrender complete control of all aspects of our lives. This actually should have been placed in the #1 slot, but you might have rebelled and not read further. All too often, through our own actions or inaction, we derail the purpose and fulfillment God has designed for our lives. God has promised the abundant life and He never fails to keep His promises – when we let Him!

10. Make this A Habit!

I hope that by now you are encouraged, or at least intrigued enough to at least be willing to try one more time. All I can say is "What have you got to lose?" **And this is square one – where you really begin**. I made a "before and after" list of what I was, what I had, and what my attitude was before I got to the end of myself. When you allow God to fully take the driver's seat, sit back, relax, and enjoy the ride! If you are willing to start the engine, He'll direct the rest. **IT'S YOUR TURN NOW!**

"Start Your Engine" Checklist

The items on the next page are to help you resolve today to take the steps necessary to begin! Using this list as an example, create an inventory with *your* "before" and "after" attitudes. Be candid as to what qualities, habits, or behaviors you would like to conquer. Don't just list the negative qualities. Be sure to list the "after" solution that will help you get there! Use these common pitfalls to identify attitudes and behaviors that may be holding you back. Be honest, but don't "judge" yourself here.

BEFORE: Note the obstacles you need to remove

* Fear of _____

* Needing approval _____

* Bad habits (drinking, smoking etc.)_____

* Dwelling on past hurt and resentment_____

* Negative self-talk_____

* Stop thinking of self, self, self!_____

* Playing the blame game _____

* Unforgiveness_____

* Worry, worry, worry! _____

* Anxiety (job, relationships, children)_____

* Perfectionism_____

* Laziness, procrastination, etc._____

* Critical attitude _____

* Apathy _____

* Other _____

AFTER: (Learning to breed success!)

...What I know I must do *first:*

...Begin a healthy lifestyle routine (eating, exercise).

...Forgive if I can — if not, ask God to take it.

...Begin to speak only what is good on purpose!

...Seek to help others who need help more

...Take full responsibility NOW; the past is over!

...Start each day with a clean slate — for self & others!

...Stop the mind games and traps upon first awareness!

...Fearlessly pursue one old dream.

...Learn the balance of activity and resting.

....Prioritize critical issues, don't sweat the small stuff.

...Ask others to help and delegate

....Seek professional help if needed

....Begin regular time of prayer and Bible study

Although this "before and after" checklist is just the overview of the "beginning," this is where it all starts – taking that first step with determination. The old saying that "what you don't know can't hurt you" is far from true! Just because you don't know you have a disease, doesn't mean you won't die if you don't get treatment! Just because you don't know your house has termites doesn't mean it won't eventually cave in, when it could have been prevented! You may not know the plan for your life, the true purpose for which you were created, or how to use the gifts and talents that you know you DO have! But how can we throw it all away and settle for mediocrity? Or worse yet, to spend this one glorious, abundant life that God has promised and not EVER know or experience HIS awesome plan for us! What a shame if we were allowed to look back and see what we might have been! God never intended for us to live lives of regret.

Whatever your "list" of limitations and changes you'd like to make, the race is beginning. And you are only in competition with one – the <u>old</u> you that has listened to the lies from the pit of hell! Can you defeat that enemy? You can, if you'll start the engine and get in the passenger seat. The Master is waiting!

Key Points to Remember:

1. Don't compare yourself to others! Only compare yourself to YOU, yesterday.

2. The strongest people ASK for help! If your friend were to come to you, you would be glad to help. Allow yourself the same!

3. Keep positive notes and scripture posted all around you. You CAN re-train yourself to begin thinking in a positive way!

4. Keep a checklist and reminder notes at all times. In a proactive way, this will MAKE you read what you were doing and thus encourage yourself to keep going, even in the most difficult situations. This preparation is the training ground for the crisis times. Even as we saw the horrifying devastation recently in New York and Washington, DC, my first reaction was to pray, pray, pray!

Four

STUMBLING BLOCKS TO STEPPING STONES

I tell you the truth, if you have faith as small as a mustard seed, you can say to this mountain, 'Move from here to there' and it will move. Nothing will be impossible for you.   *—Matthew 17:20*

Kites rise highest against the wind – not with it.
          —Winston Churchill

From my experience as a University instructor teaching teachers in a graduate program, and also teaching students in a public high school, I came to realize that adults are no different than children, when it comes to motivation, self–confidence, and coping skills! When I developed a new curriculum for a course I wanted to teach in high school entitled *Interpersonal Communication Skills,* I told the teachers in my evening class at the University about it. Just as I suspected, they wanted me to give them all the material to use for themselves!

For years as a troubled teen, and later as a virtually non–functioning, young married woman, I thought that I was the only one who was so out of control! It seemed to me that everybody else had their lives in order. They appeared to be so happy and in charge of every aspect of their day–to–day life. At the time, I had never heard the terms "dysfunctional family" or co-dependency. In the early 1970's, I had never been exposed to self-help groups, 12-Step programs, or recovery centers. The only experiences I had with psychiatrists were when my poor parents had taken me to a child psychologist out of desperation. Then in college, when I slit my wrists the first time, my roommate called the emergency hotline and they rushed me to the student medical center. Both times I "played games" with the doctors, made up stories that I thought they wanted to hear, invented great visual images for the Rorschach tests, and even underwent hypnosis in the latter case. I didn't have stumbling blocks – I had Mt. Everest to climb! Or so I thought. When the problems are your own, they are magnified to the extreme!

Some of you reading this right now may feel as I did, that it is just easier to give up than to try to go back and undo all the past and re-do what you should have done in the first place. It may seem even harder to look at all the obstacles in your life and to sincerely believe that you can overcome them! I know that as a teenager I *was* the worst problem in my parents' life. They had two other children, two "good" children who were doing what they were supposed to do, and my parents would simply lie awake all night wondering where I was this time and when that dreaded phone call would come in the middle of the night! You may be facing similar fears with a loved one, a friend, or perhaps yourself. You may be trying to break free from habits or addictions, or overcome financial problems. You may be facing physical challenges or health issues over which you have no control. Or you may simply feel guilty over what you should have done, should be doing, or even WANT to do, but don't know how!

The four areas that follow, helped me the most, in retrospect, to get started in turning my life around. I have used the strategies with both teens and adults to help them take a realistic look at their circumstances, and, to the best of their ability, to be objective. If you get stuck trying to assess the following, again be bold enough to ask a close friend or loved one to give you an honest answer.

Step 1: Chipping Away the Stumbling Blocks

From your past list of Obstacles to be Removed, you must now PRIORITZE. Select the ONE that you would first choose if you could only be free from one! Then select the second, third, etc. until they are in order of importance. If you think of one you may have left out, add it also. You are no longer going to see these as obstacles, but as stepping stones you can get past! It doesn't matter at this point whether these issues are real, or if you simply perceive them to be. If they affect you, you need to deal with them. Examples: "I hate my job" may be an annoyance for some, while others may have panic attacks at the thought of going to work. This is for YOU to assign the order of importance. Being overweight may be the last of your concerns, but for the anorexic or bulimic the rest of their life could be out of control because of this one issue!

Take time to really "brainstorm" and be as honest as you can. Remember that this is for YOUR benefit. No one else need ever see your list of stumbling blocks, unless you choose to share it! You can even include specific names of people who may not have been listed on your "obstacles" list – remember either the real, or the perceived! It could be family members, co-workers, friends, or even yourself. Your obstacle may seem trivial, but if it is in the slightest way keeping you from advancing, then it is worth confronting! It is time to take off the mask and get real! You can be free! IT'S YOUR TURN NOW!

MY PRIORITIZED LIST OF STUMBLING BLOCKS
The Lord orders our steps!

_____

_____

_____

_____

_____

_____

_____

_____

_____

Step 2: Identify Fears

Whenever I speak to church groups, whether it is a weekend ladies retreat, men's prayer breakfast, teen group or senior citizens, the number one prayer request by far has to do with FEAR! Whether it is a specific fear (such as fear of heights) or a general fear (such as fear of failure), I am convinced that most people, even strong Christians, are gripped by the enemy's greatest tool – **FEAR**. The old saying rings true – "all we have to fear is fear itself." We have heard the statistic that 90% of what you fear will happen never does,

5% doesn't really matter, and the remaining 5% that does happen is something you can't do anything about anyway. Yet we waste time, energy, and even our health, struck with fear and worry. Eleanor Roosevelt wrote in her autobiography, "You gain strength, courage and confidence by every experience in which you really stop to look fear in the face… You must do the thing you think you cannot do."

It isn't enough just to be aware of our fear, but how do we actually deal with it, combat it and eventually overcome it? Many do this through years of therapy or even in extreme cases actually being institutionalized. Some say it's as simple as "whistling a happy tune" or reciting positive thoughts. For me and for the hundreds I have interviewed who have overcome fears such as agoraphobia, claustrophobia, or simply fear of failure, it isn't enough to just get rid of the fear, it must actually be replaced by something of greater strength.

Take the analogy my husband always uses. As a chemist, he used to get so frustrated with me when I would try to remove stains from fabric, or carpet, or upholstery without taking into account what the stain actually was. He would always say, "Don't you know to fight fire with fire?" I didn't really understand that until my brother-in-law, who is a forester would actually start controlled fires to meet the raging fires sweeping through the forests. By the time one fire met the next, they extinguished each other because there was nothing left to burn. My husband would remind me that to remove an oil-based stain you must use oil. If the stain was water based, you remove it with water. One of my favorite scriptures comes from 2 Timothy:

God has not given us the spirit of fear but of power, and of love and a sound mind.
—2 Timothy 1:7 (KJV)

So if fear doesn't come from God and He gives us faith to combat it, then His provision for replacing it really isn't up to me. I may not have the power to overcome my fears, my insecurities, and my own inadequacies, but I truly believe He does! And "greater is He that is in me, than he that is the world"! So I give myself permission to *feel* the initial fear when it comes. After all, some fear is for good! I *want* to have that rush of adrenaline and be able to run, if a wild animal is attacking me (and I did just that a few months ago in Africa!). I want to have that surge of fear if a loved one needs me to call 911 (and I did just that when my 78-year old dad collapsed in front of me last month – fortunately, it was due to a new prescription and he is now fine again!). But, I don't want the "spirit of fear" for that is NOT from God! I don't want to be incapacitated in everyday conversations, or when meeting strangers, or when seeking a new job, or when speaking in public. And since I know I have the power, love, and sound mind from Almighty God Himself, I need not fear fear. Fear helped me learn the power of prayer!

The turning point for overcoming fear is to fight fear with faith. More on this later! At this point, simply take a 30 second "fear" inventory. Using your past lists, jot down quickly everything you can think of, without dwelling on the reason or the solution for now. Twenty-five years ago my fears included: fear of living; sometimes fear of dying; fear of flying; fear of heights; fear of failing; fear of losing control; fear of speaking in public; fear of making wrong decisions; fear of not being a good teacher; fear of not being a good wife; fear of having a baby; fear of disappointing my family; fear that I would never stop smoking, drinking, or lose weight; fear of sharing my faith with others; and so on. I think you get the picture. Be honest, don't judge.

LIST OF FEARS

_____

_____

_____

_____

_____

_____

_____

_____

_____

   If we are truly candid, those of us who are willing to share how we have overcome our "fears" will also admit we still get occasional "butterflies in the stomach" or that surge of adrenaline when facing certain situations. But the good news is that we can use that as a helpful tool in moving us ahead on the issue, instead of holding us back. That is turning a stumbling block into a stepping stone! For instance, once I would take a greyhound bus a thousand miles before I would fly. Or out of desperation if I HAD to fly, I would get drunk and spend several hours in the lavatory vomiting! Today, my husband and I have flown all around the world, including flying in a mail plane to the Arctic

Circle; flying on a 3-seat prop plane to the remote Okavango Delta in Botswana (where there wasn't even an air strip – much less an airport). We have hired private planes several times, once from Emu Airlines in southern Australia to fly to Kangaroo Island, once to get from Hong Kong to Malaysia, because we were in "the neighborhood," and once to get out of a mudslide in Costa Rica. I even parasailed over Acapulco and took a hot air balloon ride over an Aborigine village in the Outback of Australia.

Now you may think these were foolish risks and you would never do any of them. I am not advocating that you do anything you don't WANT to do. But I never want to forget the entire year that I spent virtually captive as a recluse in a little three-room apartment. I couldn't get a job, didn't want to go out in public, had no friends, and I spent every day lying on the sofa, eating, drinking, smoking pot, and cursing the day I was born.

MY ONLY FEAR TODAY IS NOT FULFILLING GOD'S PURPOSE FOR MY LIFE!

Step 3: Move Beyond Fear

So the real question regarding each of your listed fears is how do you get from being overwhelmed by that fear into getting to the place where you don't even think of it anymore? Did I wake up one morning and get off a greyhound bus from Alabama to St. Louis, and directly hop on Singapore Air to the Orient? Did I find a miracle diet that instantly took off those 100 pounds I needed to lose? Did I go from sitting on a bar stool discussing divorce with my husband to celebrating 30 years together, the last ten of which have been more exciting, more romantic, and more fulfilling than ever? Of course not! And I didn't even sit down and make a list of each "baby step" of change I needed to make (although in retrospect that might have been very helpful!) Instead, as I was honestly aware of each of my inadequacies, my weaknesses, my bad habits, my negative thoughts, I began to actively DO what I knew I should – **whether I wanted to, or not.** Faith is stepping out in the midst of fear and taking the necessary action, whether you *feel* like it or not!

When I was a rebellious teen, I thought nothing of taking ridiculous, even dangerous risks. I would compete in drinking contests. Other times I would see how high the speedometer on my parents' car could go (120 mph was the highest that I remember). I have already shared my horrible teen years, but the important point for each of us to learn is that what we perceive as our worst traits may be flip–flopped into our greatest assets.

The goal here is to be aware of the personality traits that you may have considered your "weaknesses." Maybe these were the things that used to get you in trouble at home or school, or things you see so clearly in others that you wish you could overcome. Examples: You may feel trapped by shyness, or you are intimidated by others, or you can't begin a conversation, you talk too much or too little, have to have the last word, you may be disorganized (that's my nemesis), or you may be a perfectionist, or overly emotional, apathetic, can't say no, too self-centered, can't trust others. Now to the best of your ability, make one more "list" of anything that comes to mind that you may have previously omitted from your weaknesses and your strengths. In the next chapter we will look closely at strategies to turn the weaknesses around, or at least find ways to cope, get help, or actually use these as "assets" in ways you may never have thought! I can finally admit my weaknesses and try to learn from them. If I am unable to reverse a weakness, I try to learn a coping strategy for it! Remember that it is often very easy for us to find fault and catalogue weaknesses that we have.

Strengths sometimes prove harder to list. Instead of spending so much time and energy trying to overcome weaknesses, we will look at ways to use and capitalize on your greatest strengths. You may think they are useless talents because they come so naturally to you. Believe me, I know the traits I most admire in others are those I lack and have struggled with for years: people who are disciplined, organized, have administrative gifts, are even tempered, people who can cook, who maintain beautiful gardens, who think logically, and I could list many more! I am *none* of these! That is why I not only admire these qualities in others, but also must depend on my family and friends and co-workers who possess these talents. So be thorough in listing your strengths, as they may be less apparent, but are nonetheless very important. IT'S YOUR TURN NOW!

MY WEAKNESSES

MY STRENGTHS

My father once gave me the wise advice, "Whatever you think about doing, do just the opposite!" I STILL THINK ABOUT THAT STATEMENT! I know my "old" nature, and I still know what my weaknesses and shortcomings are. In these areas I am resolved that for the rest of my life, although it gets easier and easier as time goes on, I will still have to DO the opposite of what I WANT to do in some areas. I have to still battle some tendencies. For instance, I still have the old "If it feels good, do it" nature. I hate to admit it, but I still occasionally want to go on eating binges at all the greasy, fast food places I used to drive thru and then go home and lie on the sofa and do nothing! But I know how horrible I will feel, how much time I will waste, what it will do to my body, and how I will beat myself up with guilt. More than anything, I have already asked God to take over this old habit and I trust HIM! So against my *feelings* and *selfish desires*, I make myself eat something healthy and fulfilling. I go for a walk whether I *feel* like it or not. Or perhaps I will read something inspirational, pray, write letters, or do something worthwhile, instead of falling asleep on the sofa watching soap operas and waking up to a food hangover and start the cycle all over again. I did this for too many wasted years. Thank God for delivering me!

I DIDN'T KNOW HOW TO LIVE A BALANCED LIFE, AND I COULDN'T IMAGINE HOW MUCH FREEDOM THERE IS IN DOING SO!

"Let us not be weary in well doing: for in due season we shall reap, if we faint not."

Galatians 6:9

Being willing to make changes requires some real honesty. Taking into consideration the strengths, gifts, talents, and desires you have, ask yourself what you are *willing* to change, to give up, or alter in order to achieve that dream or goal you know you are meant to achieve? First, get a clear picture of that "dream" which you may have put on the back burner. If you had no fear of failing, no financial restraints, and no circumstances to keep you from succeeding, where and what would you be doing? Don't be vague; don't just say you would like to have a happy family and a nice house and a nice job. Be very specific and begin to take a look at the "pros and cons."

Two years ago I had to make such a decision when my retirement year from teaching arrived. Did I really want to retire? I loved my students and I loved the classes I taught. I was involved in such fulfilling student projects like peer mediation and conflict resolution. We were initiating a new Alternative School for students who had been suspended or were failing, or dropping out. I loved these at-risk teens, and I was thrilled to work with them, since I had been one of them growing up! I sponsored the before school prayer group, the Drama Club (with over 100 student members), and I had been directing the school plays and musicals for 25 years. My marriage was great, I was in good health, my family was loving and supportive, and I couldn't have asked for more!

But... don't you hate it when things seem to be great, *but*.... I know I shouldn't feel this way, *but*.... If you have ever had that longing stirring within for something that you aren't even sure what it is, *but*... you know that way down deep in your spirit there is something else – something more. As my husband and I mulled over the opportunities, and as my students begged me NOT to retire, I found it hard to even think about it. *But*... the radio station where I had been part–time for three years, wanted me to go full–time. A producer from a local television station called to see if I wanted to do a weekly segment. Webster University, where I had been occasionally teaching, developed a new course they wanted me to teach. My first principal from 1973 strolled into my classroom and told me he was retiring from the speaking circuit, wanted me to speak around the country, and he and his wife would mentor me. Was this all an amazing coincidence or "a sign?" Or perhaps a "test?"

Instead of spending our lives waiting for signs, wondering what God's will is for us, or even just blindly jumping from risk to risk, the first real key to making changes is to take action. And the first action is to identify the one area you would most LIKE to change if you could. Look back over your list and choose that TOP priority to begin. It will be easy in some areas to make a pro/con list to see IF YOU SHOULD make that change. For instance, "Should I lose weight?" Perhaps you are 10 or more pounds over your desired weight (remember I was 100+ lbs. overweight!). I didn't have any reasons why I should NOT lose weight! I had high blood pressure, I had trouble breathing, I was depressed, lethargic, and had a hundred reasons why I SHOULD lose weight! But I couldn't do it alone. I had tried *everything!*

You may have an area such as my decision of whether to retire from teaching and launch a new career or remain a few more years. Or you may have a serious decision to make over what to do with a rebellious child, or how to deal with a marital problem, or whether to make a move for personal or professional reasons. To help me make the decision whether or not to retire, my husband and I made a constructive list of the "pros" and "cons." Select your most urgent concern at this point in your life and begin a PRO & CON list regarding this issue. Remember none of this is set in stone and you may change elements as you move forward, gain new insight, or have further circumstances change, but this is where to BEGIN – to take action and get the process going! IT'S YOUR TURN NOW!

MY FIRST ISSUE FOR CHANGE

TO _____ *or_NOT TO* _____

LIST ALL THE REASONS FOR (PRO)

_____

_____

_____

_____

_____

_____

_____

LIST THE REASONS AGAINST (CON)

_____

_____

_____

Five

SCRAP IT OR REBUILD?

Have no fear of sudden disaster or the ruin that overtakes the wicked, for the Lord will be your confidence and will keep your foot from being snared.
                                        —*Proverbs 3:25–26 (NIV)*

The hardest thing in life to learn is which bridge to cross and which to burn.   —*David Russell*

I am known to be one of the biggest pack–rats in the world. I used to literally save EVERYTHING! I inherited the "I might need it someday" trait – from my mother and my grandmother! My grandmother died at the beautiful age of 99, having been the oldest living graduate of the University of Missouri School of Journalism, Class of 1919. She kept a diary her entire life. Her attic, basement, closets, and entire house were filled with memorabilia. Her keepsakes contained some very valuable vintage and antique items, some treasures that were meaningful and sentimental to the family, and some things we still haven't figured out why she kept them (wrapping paper and balls of string and giant wads of tinfoil and mateless shoes). My mother on the other hand (who claims she isn't "eccentric," just highly unique), wanted to be a fashion designer before she left college in 1945 to marry my dad who served in the Navy during WW II. She became a decorator and costumer for a local theater guild and began amassing enormous quantities of turn of the century costumes, mannequins, and masks. She somehow incorporated her acquisitions into the decorating scheme of the traditional ranch home she and Dad built in the 1950's. When my friends spent the night at our home, if they awoke in the middle of the night to use the bathroom, they would have a shock when they encountered life–sized mannequins in the hallway. But my siblings and I got used to it.

When on a whim Mom painted the exterior of our home bright purple, no one in our hometown thought it strange, since that is the only color she ever wears. I grew up on garage sales and flea markets and was so grateful that I was prepared to be a drama teacher. Of the fifty plays and musicals I directed or starred in, I always had Mom for every prop or costume we could possible need. If not, she certainly knew where to find them!

I share this anecdotal story because it illustrates the source of my irrational "pack-ratting"! However, *I* alone must be the determining factor in overcoming it. Some of you would have no trouble in choosing from the following options for solving this dilemma.

POSSIBLE OPTIONS:

1. Take all the junk, memorabilia from 25 years of teaching, 30 boxes of saved mail from radio listeners and television viewers, all the stored costumes and props and saved clothes ranging from size 6 to 26, and everything else, and one by one, pitch it, store it, use it or file it away!

2. Hire someone else to sort through all of this, categorize it, and decide what to throw away and what should be kept. (At least there would be less work for me!)

3. Build a hidden storage room in my house where no one can see all my junk and at least buy myself enough time to divide it into categories, put each in boxes to be labeled, and store it all away out of sight.

4. Go through and find the items that would be meaningful to family, friends, former students, etc. Give these away as "love gifts" for them to keep as memorabilia.

5. Sift through and locate the most valuable items. Take the remaining stuff and rent a booth in a local antique mall. At least make some money from it.

6. Invite your mother (or others who love this process) to help you sort and go through all the items. Make it a meaningful and shared experience - even reminiscing!

7.   Have massive garage sales until all is sold and at least have something to show for it.

8. Give everything that can truly be used by someone, to a local charity or your church mission's pantry. If in doubt, let them throw it out.

9. Wrap the valuable items and give them away for birthday or Christmas gifts. Include the story behind them. This makes the gift very unique.

10. Have a giant bonfire and burn it all!

I must confess… the truth is…I have done all of the above – several times – except for #10, which in retrospect, is what I should have done in the first place!

Although all this may sound like a humorous anecdote to you, for my family and those who are closest to me, they are all too aware that this is a real problem! I am known by these affectionate titles: "the bag lady," "the big purse lady," and the "junquette" (when my friends want to be really kind). The truth is that I waste so much time looking for things, organizing, sorting, filing, boxing, wrapping, re-doing what could have been done in half the time, that it's one of my largest day–to–day frustrations!

I don't intend to be flippant in using this illustration. This may seem trivial to you when you are perhaps faced with rebuilding your entire life after the death of a loved one, or after a painful divorce, or deciding how to deal with suddenly being out of work, or the frustration of seeking the right job, or school, or career change. But the decision making process is the same! What is the best approach? Do we "scrap it," "rebuild it," or some blend of the two? The ten-step analysis I used above for myself may be the "model" to determine the appropriate tactic.

Step 1: Take Inventory

This is where you literally "take inventory" of the situation. What do you have left (physically or otherwise) that you WANT to keep from the failed marriage, from the deceased loved one, from your past job, etc. Be careful not to throw the baby out with the bath water!

Step 2: Get An Impartial Perspective

Is there someone who is not too close to the situation that could help you analyze or sort through this on an impartial basis? You may or may not have to "hire" this particular person as it could be a pastor, a teacher, counselor, or someone you may find in the yellow pages!

Step 3: Build in Time: Go Forward at a Realistic Pace

You may simply need to give yourself a little time – for peace of mind. Make sure it's a wise or healthy use of time. If you find you are using this as an excuse to isolate or procrastinate, that is a different story. But if this is something you can "store away" so to speak, until you are prepared to deal with it, that may be very helpful! Give yourself permission to do so when appropriate!

Step 4: Share the Load

There may truly be close family members and friends who would love to help you "carry the burden" and could literally help to ease some of your pain. Again, there is a fine line between receiving help and being co-dependent! And beware of the other extreme, the "martyr trap" of believing you don't ever need help from anyone at all!

Step 5: Find a "Market"

My favorite saying that I have witnessed to be true time after time is, "Wherever you have been hurt the most is where God can use you the most." Once a grief–stricken person is able to work through at least some of the pain, there is no one who is better able to help someone going through a similar situation. This will be "valuable" for them so to speak. An alcoholic is encouraged so much by one who has "been there" and is now living a sober, fulfilled life. I have found my experience as a troubled teen has been instrumental in guiding adolescents. The gifts of hope and encouragement are powerful, especially from someone with credibility!

Step 6: Make it Meaningful!

This is actually an extension of the last step, but we will

take this a step further. A few years ago after the Columbine tragedy, I interviewed as in-studio guests on my radio program two Columbine students and their parents who were all relatives of Rachel Scott, one of the girls tragically murdered that day in Littleton, Colorado. They were visiting St. Louis to present a program called "Tragedy to Triumph." In talking about and dealing with the tragic event, they also applied lessons in how to overcome the worst events of our lives. Their experience can be related to potential situations that might be similar. Instead of dwelling on their own grief, these incredible people were able to use their tragic experience to help others. They turned the tragedy of Columbine into something positive that would have a meaningful effect on others. Millions have since read their story, heard them speak, and witnessed true healing – even the good that came out of such a horrible nightmare!

Step 7: What is It Worth?

The "marketing" aspect of my analogy may not be relevant here, but the idea that "one man's junk is another man's treasure" often applies. If your particular issue, or baggage, is something that you could use as a valuable tool of shared experience, you may find that there is a "market," so to speak, where you could help. I often think of some of my past interviews where those who have gone through what seemed like impossible situations, either wrote a book, began a foundation, a scholarship program, or ministry *because of* a related disaster in their own life! Who might your "story" bless, if told?

The parents of Amy Biehl, the American Fulbright Scholar who was savagely murdered during political violence in apartheid South Africa, were unknown, ordinary people prior to their daughter's death. They resolved to honor their daughter's memory and her life by not letting the tragedy of Amy's death overshadow the good that Amy did while in South Africa. Today, Peter and Linda Biehl operate a foundation in their daughter's name to combat and reverse the social conditions in South Africa that made violence prevalent and that resulted in their daughter's death. The Biehls have reconciled with Amy's murderers and even *employ* them today in their charitable projects! We all possess a great capacity to turn tragedy to triumph by God's grace.

Step 8: Sort and Toss

This is the point where you must decide if you want to let any or all aspects of your issue go – really "scrap it" or simply "rebuild" using valuable parts. Sometimes there is another resource you haven't explored. There just might be someone else who knows someone that could not only help you, but might have a connection or an idea beyond everything else that you have explored. You might continue "sorting" for a solution.

Perhaps you think you have done everything humanly possible, yet there still seems to be no real answer. You might be at the point where you simply "let go and turn it all over to someone else," which sounds easy. But if you decide to "toss" it, be prepared for a longer process than you may imagine. But still be open to an unperceived answer that may seem to come "out of the blue."

Step 9: Something to Show For It!

If you can creatively devise a way to "distribute" your pain or past problem to help someone who may not even know what they need, you will both be helped. I think of a former student who was virtually incapacitated with juvenile rheumatoid arthritis. She became an "overcomer" by volunteering her time as a clown at Children's Hospital and telling her story of encouragement. She is now a pre–school teacher in spite of her illness. She "wraps" her gift and gives it away!

I also think of a friend who battled depression and panic attacks after an abortion that she had never told anyone about – not even her husband. She now volunteers at a local teen pregnancy center and shares her story with those facing pregnancy, as well as those dealing with the aftermath of abortion.

Step 10: Burn or Leap (but make sure you've looked!)

This last option is truly a viable option. But don't jump in too hastily and make sure you really want to "burn all the old bridges." I know those who have. Some have cut all ties to the past and successfully started over in all aspects of their life! Others did and wished they hadn't. Whatever model you choose, just make sure you are not held captive by the past. Often, we allow our inability to make a decision paralyze us ("paralysis of analysis") from doing the things we should to make needed change. Analyze carefully, seek objective perspectives, use your gut instincts, and then get on with it.

As for me, I'm still wading through the muddle of a few more boxes to sort, but I am glad Iexperienced all these steps. I would have missed out on valuable shared experiences with friends and family and so many opportunities to bless others. I might have forgotten just how weak I am in some areas and how much I depend on God and the people He blesses me with – because they have the invaluable resources and gifts I need. And perhaps they need to share them! NOW IT'S YOUR TURN!

Using this 10-step outline process, identify the area you would like most to work through. With this needed change in mind, brainstorm each point and ask others to help as you feel comfortable. You will be amazed at the endless possibilities and new insight you will discover!

1. **Take Inventory:**

2. **Get an Impartial Perspective:**

3. **Build in Time and Pace it:**

4. **Share the Load:**

5. **Find a "Market:"**

6. **Make it Meaningful:**

7. **What is It Worth?**

8. **Sort and Toss:**

9. **Something to Show forIit:**

10. **Burn It or Leap:**

Six

WHO NEEDS A COACH?

Two are better than one for they have a good return for their work: if one falls, his friend can help him up. But pity the man who falls and has no one to help him up!
                                        —Ecclesiastes 4:9–10

Few people are successful unless a lot of other people want them to be.   *—Charles Brower*

Basketball fans around our state were amazed every year when our little rural school, Clopton High (42 in my graduating class) seemed to always send a winning team to district or state! We consistently defeated teams from much larger schools, and everyone always asked why!

When I went to the University of Alabama in 1968, I was compelled to become a football fan, because there was nothing more important than the Saturday games when the Crimson Tide was typically victorious! What did these two different teams, different sports, different locations, different size schools have in common that made them both winners? One thing – an amazing coach! Bob Wilhoit may not be a name you have ever heard, but in the 1960's and 1970's he was celebrated around the state of Missouri, receiving numerous awards for his coaching ability in high school basketball. You may be more familiar with the name Coach Paul "Bear" Bryant. His legend still lives on. Can one coach, one person, really make all the difference? **YES!**

No one would deny the importance of a fitness trainer if you truly want to get into shape. And there was a time in history when apprenticeships were the only way to learn a profession or trade – from a master. Is having a coach, a mentor, a trainer any less valuable today? As a teacher, I couldn't begin to imagine what would happen if I simply said to my students, "You can learn all of this on your own. Here's the grammar textbook, now just do it." Admittedly, there are a few high school students who could learn very well on their own and just might have the perseverance and self–discipline to stay on track, on time, and not be distracted by the rest of the class. But I also know from experience what would happen if there were no teacher, coach, or encourager there. MOST of them would "do their own thing" – and we won't even discuss what all that might include! But there is an important lesson in each of these analogies:

YOU CAN MEMORIZE THE BOOK AND ANSWER ALL THE RIGHT QUESTIONS, BUT CAN YOU SINGLE–HANDEDLY APPLY IT IN YOUR LIFE?

Your first thought may be that you would rather do it by yourself. I admit I had some students who worked much better alone – at least when reading, writing, or creating something. But when it came to cooperative learning, group work, or doing a team project, they were completely lost! Here are the reasons you should consider having someone to "coach" you. Call it having a mentor, an instructor, a trainer, a confidant, or just a supporter – but everyone needs someone. I thought I was the exception. I learned the hard way that I needed help. Now I am usually the "coach" or the one telling others to find someone!

COACHING CRITERIA

1. Strength in Numbers!

Two heads are better than one. Think about it… you have twice the ideas, usually different perspectives, and twice the experience. Don't limit this to just one coach or mentor. You could have several separately or even a group who supports you.

2. Who is Doing It?

If you know someone who is doing what you want to be doing, find out how they got there and go down the same road! Make sure when you are following a leader that they also have the same values you do and that their "path" is the way you want to achieve that goal. The end does NOT always justify the means!

3. Who is Doing It Well?

Since someone else is willing to help you overcome obstacles they have already been though and tell you strategies that did and didn't help them, why waste time re–inventing the proverbial wheel? If I want to learn to swim, but I am afraid of the water, first of all I want a coach who is a good swimmer, who is gentle and patient, but who ultimately will get me swimming!

4. Be Accountable!

Accountability is a necessity these days. The issue has been highly publicized by all the moral scandals in the news. But on a personal level, to whom are you accountable? Hopefully if you are a parent or a spouse or a child, you feel accountable to your family. If you are an employee, you should be accountable to whoever is above you. I believe that first and foremost, I am accountable to God and His moral law. So, if we really want change badly enough in a certain area of our life, we must seek an "accountability partner" to get us on track and help keep us there.

5. Discipline Yourself!

We all need both boundaries and encouragement. When I set rules of discipline in my classroom, I posted both the consequences for broken rules and the positive reinforcement, if the rules were consistently followed. I know this may not seem like a current parallel, because you are probably out of school, but we are always in the "school of life" – and each of us has a few areas that are harder to follow! But if we discipline ourselves, the rewards are great and we'll achieve our goals! Obedience is better than sacrifice!

We must learn that no matter what our past, no matter how great or how horrible our parents were, no matter what childhood tragedies or successes we may have experienced, we are responsible for NOW! Our past may *explain* why we are like we are, but it doesn't *excuse* it! And it can't prevent us from being the person we want to be! "I can do all things through Christ who strengthens me!"

However you decide to do it, formally or informally, professionally or personally, you must hook up with someone who is successful at doing what you want. It's not a big secret – the successful person has developed traits and habits that the unsuccessful person simply has not – yet! Here are some proven principles to follow:

1. Decide you will <u>not</u> be a martyr, that you will not do it alone, that you **will** seek help!

2. Seek out a person or group that best fits your need and their time. (Don't be discouraged if you ask someone who doesn't have time to be a personal mentor. They

still may be able to offer you snippets of advice or sources that helped them!)

3. Decide whether you have the resources to obtain a "paid" coach and if that best suits your needs. If not, you may be more comfortable with a support group.

4. Have your mentor, coach, or support group help you set definite goals. Create a purposeful mission statement and even set timelines for achieving your goals where applicable.

5. Divide the long-range goal into small, attainable steps. Be practical. Don't try to climb your "Everest" in one step or overnight. View the beginning from the end.

6. Commit to the long-term, but focus on the day-to-day objectives. Be realistic. I love the idea of losing 20 pounds in two weeks. But it didn't happen! I only lost one pound a week when I was losing weight! But that was 52 pounds over the course of a year and it took me two years to lose over 100 pounds. But I am in the 1% of people who have been able keep off 100 pounds for at least twenty-five years! Patience and help pay off!

7. Help your coach/group come up with meaningful short–term rewards as means of encouragement. You know what helps the most in your own circumstances, given your own personality.

8. Determine when you will be facing the toughest times in this process and be proactive in planning, so that you will be prepared to face them in advance. For

example, if you know the anniversary of the death of a loved one is going to be very difficult, make plans to go somewhere or be with another friend or loved one on that day. Plan something to keep from dwelling on your grief.

9.   Lastly, a mentor, group, coach, or instructor who is impartial and perhaps not part of your intimate personal life, may be more effective in keeping you on track professionally. But also include in the process a close friend or relative who will support you emotionally. There was a time when I didn't want anyone to know my personal feelings, inadequacies, or problems. Whether it was pride, or not wanting to impose on others, it was these attitudes keeping me from sharing my experiences with others I didn't know. But I learned that when I am honest about my shortcomings, I have family, friends, and even strangers who *want* to help, who want to support and encourage me. And I want to do the same for them!

10   Above all, have a trusted prayer partner who will keep you connected to the greatest Counselor!

IT'S YOUR TURN NOW!

USING YOUR PAST LISTS, BRAINSTORM IDEAS FOR FINDING A SOURCE OF HELP FOR THE TWO OR THREE MOST URGENT AREAS:

1.

2.

3.

Example: As a radio talk show host, one of the most tragic on-air phone calls I ever received was from a grief–stricken mother, whose son had committed suicide and she could think of no one to help her. Of course, by making a few calls we were able to find professional support groups, a pastor and church that have taken her under wing. A few more areas of help and support seemed to "appear" out of the blue. I was surrounded by sources of help for this woman. A friend's daughter had been tragically killed in a plane crash two years earlier, a co-worker lost her son suddenly a few years before, and a fellow church member, whom I didn't know well, lost her child unexpectedly from a rare disease. I asked these women if they would be willing to talk with the listener. The women all met informally in one of their homes to console, encourage, and support one an-other, sharing what has been helpful or most difficult for them. They also shared literature and books that were beneficial, and ways to tell well–meaning loved ones what you wish they would and would <u>not</u> do. This group of women has met several times since and has welcomed others who find themselves in the same situation.

*YOU MAY THINK YOU ARE ALONE, BUT THAT IS **NEVER** TRUE. ALLOW YOURSELF TO HEAL BY MOVING FORWARD **ONE MORE TIME**, EVEN IF IT TAKES ALL YOU HAVE TO TRY AGAIN!*

Seven

GETTING IN THE GROOVE

Fight the good fight of the faith. Take hold of eternal life to which you were called….
—*1 Timothy 6:12 (NIV)*

Whatever you do, or dream you can, begin it. Boldness has genius and power in it.
—*Goethe*

By this point, you have theoretically completed a lot of mental preparation, determined and listed certain goals, obstacles to overcome, and hopefully you are motivated to begin. By having taken this honest look backward and being willing to admit your weaknesses, I also hope you have candidly thought about your strengths, gifts, and talents. You should have come up with a few ideas of where you might be going from here, what changes you are ready to make, and hopefully you have a few names and ideas for those who can help you!

From this point on, you will be more motivated, more responsive to change, and will be able to be honest with your progress if you have your coach/mentor or support team staying the course with you. When you KNOW there are others who are pulling for you, who are there to cheer you on in your successes, and there to catch you when you stumble, it makes all the difference!

There are so many stories, scriptures, and parables about running the race, staying on course, not giving up, and enduring until the end. In each scenario, we often assume that those who are able to keep going with such consistency are doing so, because they are highly motivated and just won't quit. But that is not always true, and I would like to address those of you who perhaps are more like I was.

I really *wasn't* motivated in some areas for various reasons. In some circumstances, such as having over 100 pounds to lose, I felt like I had gone too far down the wrong pathway. I would have to work too hard and all I could see down the road was that I would keep trying and trying and spinning my wheels. I was afraid that once again, as I always had before, I would find myself in yet another failed attempt. When being a loser, failing, and giving up is all you have ever known, it is really hard to picture yourself as a winner or an overcomer. Even when you hear the great success stories of others and may have even personally known someone who has bounced back against all odds, you might even feel guilty that they have endured in the midst of trials far greater than yours! Perhaps you tend to think as I did. I would allow myself to go down the old negative "guilt trip" path of beating myself up even worse, all because I *didn't* have things as bad as other people. We then see others overcome so much more, and we begin the self-defeating mindset of listening to that old negative tape we run: "You ought to be ashamed of yourself; look what so-and-so did and you can't even keep going; you are a failure and always will be…" STOP THAT TAPE! Go back to your list! Henry Ford wisely said, "Whether you think that you can, or that you can't, you are usually right."

The first step in breaking that vicious cycle of self-defeatism is to be aware when that stinking thinking begins. You may not be able to PREVENT the negative thoughts from coming in the first place, but here is where you do have a choice: Scripture reminds us that God will "keep in perfect peace whose mind is stayed on Him!"

STRATEGIC BATTLE PLAN

1. When the negative thoughts pop in (and they will – so expect them), STOP! As soon as you are aware of that negative thinking... STOP! I mean right then and there, stop in your tracks and realize you are back in that rut of negative thinking. It may have been a self-defeating thought; it may consist of jealousy, anger, resentment, or frustration over a circumstance or even be directed at a person. It doesn't matter who or what, or how horrible the thought, you CAN STOP!

2. You now have the choice at this point to literally make your mouth start speaking against this negative thinking and OUT LOUD begin to say the most positive words you can. My fail–proof counter attack to this negative onslaught is to pray out loud! As soon as I catch myself thinking something negative, I thank God immediately that I am aware of this negativity, that I can stop that thought process from progressing, and I begin to praise Him for allowing me to have the capacity to literally change my mind! I may begin to recite the Lord's Prayer, or the 23rd Psalm, or sing a hymn. If this sounds crazy to you, just try it and you'll be a believer! Again I ask...what have you got to lose? In this case, the negative thinking leads you back into bondage to the same old traps you may have been locked in for years! Allow God to let you out! He's waiting!

Be not conformed any longer to the pattern of this world, but be transformed by the renewing of your mind.
                                          —*Romans 12:2 (NIV)*

What I am suggesting is that you renew your mind by doing some mental "house cleaning," by learning to sweep away all of the old clutter that keeps popping in and replace it with new, optimistic thoughts. The right attitude will inspire you to take action! Instead, of thinking how hard it will be or what will happen "if," or that you may fail again, shut out the old messages, keep the praying and singing going, and begin immediately. You will start to realize you CAN replace the old clutter with beautiful, new, permanent ideas, thoughts, goals and joy that will lead you on a new path!

SOME SAY "IT'S TOO LATE TO TEACH AN OLD DOG NEW TRICKS"...I SAY THAT GOD CAN RE–TRAIN "OLD DOGS!"

I know from personal experience that you CAN begin new habits; that you can re-learn and re-think and undo years of negative programming. I have seen people who are in their eighties turn their whole lives around! I mentioned in a previous chapter the man who learned to read at age 97 and wrote a book at 101. I have a friend who learned to swim when she was 72 and now leads a water aerobics group for senior citizens at the YMCA (By the way, she just turned 80!) We took my parents to Greece last year for their 55th wedding anniversary. And even though they are in their late seventies, they beat all of us "kids" to the summit of the Acropolis where the Parthenon overlooks Athens! Age is no longer an excuse.

PHYSICAL LIMITATIONS MAY IGNITE CREATIVITY

I know it is easy for those of us in relatively good health to say what we would or wouldn't do in certain situations. I know that I often whine over little aches and pains and have to stop that negative tape a hundred times a day when I am ill. But I also know that the most amazing and admirable people are those who have accomplished impossible feats and pursued their dreams in the midst of physical adversity.

I recently interviewed several of the contributors of a book written entirely by MS patients. One lady is still an air traffic controller and pilot; one whose dream it was to be an artist, learned to paint with the brush in her mouth when the use of her arms was gone. I also interviewed Christopher Reeve's wife Dana who told of all the extraordinary ways he is able to stay upbeat and positive. We know of a wonderful blind man who climbed Mt. Everest, a terminal cancer patient who refused to quit teaching, and many who compete in sports in their wheelchairs! One of my favorite callers on my radio program is a sweet little saintly woman who not only is in a wheelchair, but for health reasons must stay in her little apartment day after day. She has a list of "shut–ins" she calls every day to check on them, encourage them and pray for them. When she completes that list, she calls random numbers in the telephone directory and asks people if they need prayer. I marvel at her as she relates stories of people who said, "Who told you to call?" And she simply says, "I prayed that God would show me someone who needs prayer and encouragement, and I believe He did!" She has never had anyone hang up on her! By the way she is 84 years old and full of JOY!

A MIND IS A TERRIBLE THING TO WASTE!

One of my friends has been dealing with the slow, ago-nizing process of seeing her precious mother decline men-tally from Alzheimer's Disease. She realizes things her Mom says and does are beyond her control, and that sometimes she doesn't even recognize her own family. But my friend goes to visit faithfully, day after day and keeps a notebook of the positive things that occur – an unexpected hug, a past memory her Mom resurrects from forty years ago, hold-ing her hand, or praying with her. She CHOOSES to dwell on the positive and release the negative things that are be-yond her control. She prays for her mother every day before she leaves her room, whether her Mom is aware of it or not.

WE MAY NOT BE ABLE TO CONTROL WHAT HAP-PENS TO US OR AROUND US, BUT WE CAN CONTROL HOW WE CHOOSE TO REACT!

YOUR ATTITUDE DETERMINES YOUR ALTITUDE!

When we are caught up in competition or even the ev-ery day "rat–race" of life, it is hard to step back and take an honest assessment of what matters most in our life! We can be so busy and so intent on being "the winner" or being "the best" or the "richest" or the "thinnest" or "most popu-lar" that we forget what is really important in our lives – our faith, our family, our friends, forgiveness, fun! (I always use these words with students to show them that F's are not always negative!)

The converse of the overachievers and perfectionists are those who never compete, who see themselves as useless failures and unable to ever change. I admit that there are many folks whose past circumstances may have certainly given them reasons to believe this. I can identify with them. But once I have made the determination that the past is over, I admit I may not be responsible for what happened to me in the past, but I AM responsible for my future. And beginning right now, I CHOOSE to take full responsibility for my mind, body and soul – no matter WHAT pitiful state they may presently be in!

The following is an example I use in my seminars to help us take a realistic look at how we need to keep our lives balanced! Notice the size of each piece of the pie and examine the categories closely. If there are only two key ideas and goals that I want you to get out of this entire chapter, they are BALANCE AND INNER PEACE! No matter how distorted your own balance wheel might be, and no matter how little inner peace you have had in the past, you can change!

Take a minute to make an honest estimation of the proportions you would give each of these six areas in your own life. You may have even left out one or two of the pieces – don't be alarmed. I was defunct in all of them! But in the next chapter we are going to begin the process in each of these areas of seeing how to change, persevere, and keep moving forward. But first, to the best of your ability, for **each** of the six areas answer the following:

A.   Why have you allotted so much or so little to this area?

B.   Do you WANT to give more time and focus to this area, even if you don't see how?

C.   Do you feel you *should* give more to this area, even if you don't really *want* to?

Do not be conformed to this world, but be transformed by the renewing of your mind.   –*Romans 12:2*

How much would you allocate to each section of your own Life's Balance Wheel?

1. Physical:

2. Personal Growth

3. Work

4. Emotional:

5. Family

6. Spiritual

Eight

PERSEVERING THROUGH THE GROWING PAINS

Consider it pure joy, my brothers, whenever you face trials of many kinds, because you know that the testing of your faith develops perseverance, so that you may be mature and complete, lacking in nothing.

—James 1:4

Never give up, for that is just the place and time that the tide will turn.

—Harriet Beecher Stowe

Congratulations my friend! If you have made it here to Chapter 8, you are really ready this time to get on that path and the new life you KNOW you can have! If you are like I am, you may have made this declaration "to change" a thousand times before, and you may have put this book down several times and you are just now picking it up – later! But, good news! I believe sincerely that no matter how much you wish and dream and think about that new life, you have to be truly READY! Whether you are at this point out of motivation and determination that it is your time now, or if you are here out of desperation because you have no other options left, it doesn't matter. If you are *willing to be made willing*, to receive help in actually putting your thoughts and dreams into action, then roll up your sleeves and let's keep going. The preparation is half the battle, but now is where you will begin to actually see the application, the results, and be prepared for others in your sphere of influence to begin to notice! You will NOT be the same person! At my 25-year high school reunion I received the award of: **"The Most Changed!"** For me, that was the greatest compliment!

Remember your before/after list from Chapter 2? This is where it is going to be put into action. Those items from your "before" list will soon have the counterpoints in your ever–increasing "after" list! Remember three key points as we get started:

1. PERSEVERENCE

2. CONSISTENCY

3. EXPECTATIONS

The easiest way for me to persevere in the midst of something that is difficult, or challenging, or when I am emotionally attached is to simply "focus on focusing." This may involve little post it notes with motivators all over the house; it may mean asking my accountability partner (coach/mentor) to call me at certain intervals; or it sometimes involves writing a letter to myself and reading it over and over a thousand times. For instance, when I had been teaching for ten years, I knew that according to our salary chart, I was at my limit. Other teachers who had been teaching for only a few years were making more than I was, because I had not obtained my Masters degree and they had. Our school district had several levels and columns based on experience, length of service, extra curricular activities, and the biggest criteria ...advanced degrees.

I was one of those teachers who was involved in EVERYTHING at school and loved all that I was doing. But I couldn't possibly see how I could have time or energy to take any graduate level courses! I was directing the plays and musicals after school; I was the sponsor for the speech and debate team; I served on the state board for the Thespian Society; I worked with the at-risk students; I directed community theater; and I even created a new curriculum course for our district English and Writing program. I was already speaking professionally on the side and very involved in our church, our community neighborhood association, and numerous other clubs and organizations. I didn't WANT to go back to school, especially at the graduate level, because I wanted to have fun! I wanted to do what I was doing because I loved it, not because I HAD to, and certainly not just for the monetary increase (although I calculated I had already lost $50,000 by not having a Masters degree, and if I taught until retirement, it would only be A LOT more!). So I needed to follow exactly what I have been presenting to you – assess the situation realistically and weigh the pros and cons, begin to take action in increments!

DID I TRULY WANT TO MAKE THE CHANGE AT THIS POINT IN MY LIFE?

Part of me wanted to change. To be honest, the increase in money was a major incentive. I realized that younger teachers who were doing less than I was, putting in fewer hours, and not even sponsoring extra curricular activities were making more than I was. Instead of resenting them, I began to realize that I should have done what they did a long time ago! Yet, the dread of more schooling, the thought of tedious hours of studying and drudgery, and even possible failure loomed ahead.

WAS I MOTIVATED ENOUGH TO BEGIN THE CHANGE PROCESS?

I was not motivated to jump in and enroll in graduate school, but I was "willing to be made willing." I knew myself well enough through years of self-assessment that I realized I could probably accomplish the goal, but was I willing to make the sacrifice in other areas of my life in order to achieve it? I wasn't ready to "start my engine," but I was curious enough to see what entering the race would involve. I re-examined and followed the steps presented to you in Chapter 3 where I assessed my strengths and weaknesses based on this particular issue, and decided that I didn't have enough information to have a realistic picture of what would be required. I tend to lean on my "feelings" and emotions far too much, which had gotten me in plenty of trouble in the past. So my decision at this point was that I was willing to take that first "baby step," and maybe explore further options.

WHAT ACTION WAS I WILLING TO TAKE?

I scheduled an exploratory appointment with the nearest college, Webster University, to see how much time, money and energy I would have to invest, and to see if there was a course of study I might actually enjoy! (I had been on social and scholastic probation my freshman year of undergraduate school, and those old memories and tapes started racing through my head).

WHO WOULD BE MY BEST SOURCE FOR A COACH/MENTOR?

I first sought advice from those who knew me best and who would be directly impacted themselves – my husband, family, and closest friends. I then sought input from a variety of colleagues who were already in the same graduate program there, or who had completed it successfully. I even tried to find some who had "failed" or had dropped out. The only one that I could find was a fellow teacher who had to postpone his studies due to an illness in his family. Otherwise, he indicated that he would have continued. I weighed all of the "pro's and con's."

WAS I WILLING TO TAKE ANOTHER STEP FORWARD AT THIS POINT?

I determined, somewhat reluctantly, to take one class only during the summer. The course was for just one week, from 8 a.m. – 4 p.m., and I leaped out in faith and registered. I was attracted by the course's content of building relationships with a diversity of students. It sounded interesting, applicable, and even fun!

All of this information is important to note at this time, for if had I picked a course at random that hadn't fit my needs and personality, I would have been setting myself up for failure. I might have flunked or dropped out of that first graduate-level course, and never continued.

But because I had done an honest self-assessment, took

into account my strengths and weaknesses, sought advice and help, and was honest with my emotions, I was ready to at least "explore" this growth area. I followed the same procedure for all future courses in which I enrolled. I moved very slowly and cautiously, taking baby steps along the way. As I experienced measures of success, as well as many trials and errors, I was at least able to keep my focus, and I persevered. I was consistent in my approach as well in my studies. You must understand that for me, these were not two of my natural assets. Most of my life I had NOT been able to persevere and in very few things had I ever been consistent. But I had also rushed headfirst and haphazardly into things that I wanted to experience, recklessly taking negative, foolish risks. And if the gamble didn't kill me, I would rush into the next whim that came along.

In this Master's Program, I depended on the leading and wisdom and accountability of others, as well as my personal commitment to move forward in slow, small increments. My expectations were set for the here and now. Even thinking of the years, the future courses, and the expenses involved in receiving a Master's Degree were too intimidating and overwhelming. But I had successfully completed one course and I knew I could TRY one more. FOR THE NEXT YEAR OR TWO I FOLLOWED THIS STEADY, SLOW, CONSISTANT AND PERSISTENT PROCESS!

Following the Balance Wheel, I knew I needed to maintain the areas that were in proper proportion and still work on those that were not. If I didn't do that, I could go to the extreme of sacrificing health, relationships and peace of mind, just for the sake of receiving a Master's Degree. I had friends who were perfectionists, and ladder climbers, literally killing themselves, and I was not willing to play that game of insanity.

I KEPT MY BALANCE WHEEL EXPECTATIONS ON SHORT TERM GOALS:

PHYSICALLY: I kept the same three components of persistence, consistency, and short term expectations going on a day-by-day, sometimes hour-by-hour basis. I was determined to eat healthy meals. My husband and other family members were a great help here! Even if I could only do five–minute increments of exercising in spurts, I did it. Just that little boost added to my motivation. I knew I was a "zombie" after 10 p.m. at night, so I would go to bed early and get up at 5 a.m. when I could arrange study and preparation time. (I know some of you are gasping at these hours – you have to set what works for you! My husband stays up until midnight or 1 o'clock, but sleeps until 7:30 or 8:00 a.m. Some of you may need even more sleep.)

PERSONAL GROWTH: Since I considered this category filled at that time while going back to school, I only had a few other additions. I took a time-management course, which for me was a waste of time, because I have since learned I am nearly incapable of this. (I was diagnosed two years ago with adult attention deficit disorder, but that's a subject for another book!) I gradually saw this as a committed time in my life, and I realized I needed to temporarily drop a few of my other extra-curricular and social activities that weren't as high on my priority list.

WORK: I was determined that my teaching and all of my students would not suffer, because I was "moonlighting." So I found creative ways to incorporate what I was studying into my classroom curriculum. I created new units on *Oral Interpretation of Literature* as I was taking that course myself, and actually brought a few of my students into my university class to perform. I got input from my advanced students when I was in a *Curriculum Design* class and presented the survey results to my professor. I made each class fun by making it applicable to what I was really doing – not just to get the grade and the money increase (though they were my long-term motivators, I needed everyday incentives as well). My high school students and colleagues were excited to hear what I was doing and offered creative ideas – and I incorporated a few of them!

EMOTIONAL: I would love to give a glowing report here and tell you how emotionally stable I was during all of this, but my husband and family would have to tell the world what a liar I was. So I will be candid in the hopes that this will help you as well. There were times when I wanted to kill! Okay, maybe it wasn't that severe, but I was forced to learn new strategies to help me "turn off the negative tapes" and realize that my irrational thoughts were probably putting me on an emotional roller coaster! I also was going through some health problems at the time that affected me far more emotionally than physically. Just the added hours of stress and time constraints, brought me into a greater awareness of and need for the next two categories!

RELATIONSHIPS: I know that many of you going through major times of decision–making and change don't have the loving support of family and friends. So I will at this point just tell you that I was very blessed and grateful that I did have such incredible support from my loved ones. I am very sorry for those of you who don't, but that doesn't mean you can't have other supportive relationships that WILL help you, support you, and encourage you. You must be willing to seek them out and not be afraid to make the first move! I have known single moms who have literally been lifesavers for one another! I have known people who have remained best friends with those they met in a support group. Others have a distant relative, or surrogate parent, or fellow co–worker in whom they can confide. Cherish the relationships you have, and whatever is going on personally – WHAT-EVER IT TAKES – learn strategies NOT to take your frustrations out on those closest to you. Your spouse, children, family, and friends should not bear the brunt all the time. In times of real trouble when you do need to vent or just cry on a shoulder, you will find who your real friends and supporters are! Make sure you are there for them as well! By the way, this is a summary of what I have LEARNED THE HARD WAY. I am the first to admit it is easier said than done. I have learned to forgive and seek forgiveness quickly. (Do not let the sun go down on your anger!)

SPIRITUAL: This last slice of the pie is usually the first to give way, as the other five tend to take up all 24 hours of our entire day. But I also learned the hard way here. For all of my troubled teen years and on into adulthood, the "spiritual" side of life was elusive to me. I had attended Sunday School as a little girl but I was a trouble maker there as well. I got kicked out of the Christmas pageant, had to leave a week long Church camp for causing trouble, and several other such horrid memories.

Many years down the road, because I had refused to pray or even acknowledge God, I felt that if He did exist, I was not going to have anything to do with Him. After all, I had grown up with an older sister who was straight A's, popular, beautiful, and thin! I had a younger brother who was handsome, popular, and a star athlete. My parents were proud of them, but I had disgraced the family. There couldn't be a God, because life was too unfair.

Through all of my years of rebellion, torment, searching, running away, and dropping out, I had a life changing moment that was THE TURNING POINT IN MY LIFE. At age 23, on my third unsuccessful suicide attempt, I finally screamed out the word "God" for the first time in five years. I remember the helpless, frantic pathetic prayer as if it were yesterday instead of more than twenty-five years ago. I screamed, "All right, God! If you are really up there, if you are really who they say you are, then here is this pathetic, pitiful life, if you want it, because I'm ready to end it all." I only remember throwing myself onto the bed and crying myself to sleep; but when I woke up, for the first time in my life I had what I had been looking for all along! There were no burning bushes or lightning bolts, or angels, or voices. I simply had the "peace that passes all understanding." I knew that all of the old Sunday school lessons hadn't been in vain, as I remembered a portion of the Lord's prayer, and I prayed for the first time in years, to the God who had been there all along just waiting for me to come to Him.

If you have never experienced this peace, and if you don't even know how to begin to pray, remember that Jesus said to come as a little child. His own disciples didn't know how to pray and they asked him to teach them. That's when he told them to pray like this:

"Our Father, who art in Heaven, hallowed, be Thy name. Thy Kingdom come, Thy will be done, on earth as it is in Heaven. Give us this day our daily bread. And forgive us our trespasses as we forgive those who trespass against us. And lead us not into temptation but deliver us from evil. For Thine is the Kingdom, and the power and the glory forever. Amen."

Many times I have only time to say, "Lord please help me," and I know now that He always hears. Begin in this area exactly as you would in any other. Be open to seeking and searching for yourself. Try reading John, Chapter 3 for starters and just pray that God would reveal Himself to you. I had to find out if He was real, and if He was, I wanted ALL He had for my life. Not crumbs, not pieces, not just a little. I wanted ALL that He was willing to give. And I found out He had already given His all. He sent His own son to die for my PAST, present and future. I realized that all my sins were nailed to the cross with Jesus. What a revelation, and what a new life I had in Christ! I pray this portion of the balance wheel will be the key that unlocks all the other areas for you, as it certainly did for me! I received the greatest, most life-changing gift when I trusted Christ as my personal Savior!

Each one should use whatever gift he has received to serve others, faithfully administering God's grace.
                                                            1Peter 4:10

I am the loudest member of the choir when we sing, "Amazing Grace, how sweet the sound that saved a wretch like me!"

IT'S YOUR TURN NOW!

Where will you have the greatest difficulty in your first selected area to change? Tell why and what you can do, now that you know how to be proactive?

1. PERSEVERENCE

2. CONSISTENCY

3. EXPECTATIONS

<u>Answer the Same for the Following</u>:

1.   DO YOU TRULY WANT TO MAKE THE CHANGES AT THIS POINT IN YOUR LIFE?

2.   ARE YOU MOTIVATED ENOUGH TO BEGIN THE CHANGE PROCESS?

3.   WHAT ACTION ARE YOU WILLING TO TAKE IMMEDIATELY?

4.   WHO CAN YOU SEE AS YOUR BEST SOURCE OF HELP?

5.   WHAT WILL BE SUBSEQUENT STEPS TO FUR-THER ACTION YOU CAN TAKE?

LONG TERM:

SHORT TERM:

I know the plans I have for you, plans for you to prosper.
Jeremiah 29:11

Nine

ENJOYING THE RIDE 'TILL YOU GET TO WHERE YOU'RE GOING

How many of you with children have gone through the frustration of beginning a family vacation only to get the car packed, the house secured, and the family finally all buckled in the car for the long drive ahead, and then you hear those words for the first of a thousand times: "How long till we get there?" We could all write hilarious sit-coms of memories of our family trips! If we were honest, most of the memorable moments were the unexpected joys and spontaneous adventures along the way. Isn't that really how it is in our own lives as well?

One of my favorite devotional books is My Utmost for His Highest by Oswald Chambers. One of his constant themes is that life is a journey and our growth is a process. He emphasizes that God is not looking for a "perfect finished product" to use as a showcase display. He measures our progress by our heart's devotion to Him- not the good works we do. Of course, the more we grow in our relationship to Him, the more we will want to do for Him and for others. The difference is that we were once struggling and striving and trying to achieve. We were always asking, "Lord, when are we going to get there"? As with a child in the car, we can whine and question and complain, or we can enjoy the beauty of the scenery and the fellowship along the way! What He really wants is for us to enjoy the journey – and we can only do that when we have a balanced life – in our work, our relationships and our love for our Creator!

When we had the blessing of taking my parents to Greece for their 55th anniversary, we also took a cruise to a few Islands and on to Turkey. As we toured the ruins of Ephesus in Turkey, we were reminded of how Paul wrote to the new church there as well as other churches of his day, such as Rome and Corinth and Galatia. He was so frustrated with their lack of growth and their constant complaining. He knew that they were still seeking the pleasures of this world. But he also knew they were capable of change and could become overcomers, as he had become. He told them he was the "chiefest of sinners" and he had even been a Christian slayer at one time – a murderer! And yet now he was the greatest example of a truly changed life. He had personally encountered Jesus Christ on the road to Damascus where he was blinded and incapacitated and confronted with one simple question: "Why do you persecute me?" He was never the same after that, once all of the foolishness and sin of his past were made perfectly clear to him. He saw what he was, but Christ showed him what he could become. He eventually wrote, "I have learned whatever state I am in to be content." He went on to write most of the New Testament and modeled the most encouraging love relationship we can have. Isn't that what we are all really searching for in life – to be content, to be happy, to have peace and joy? Paul had found the key, and I finally did, and I pray that you have as well!

As my family toured where Mary, the mother of Jesus, lived out her final days, we were reminded of one of the last requests given to the apostle John. He fulfilled his final assignment as Jesus requested from the cross to him, "Behold thy mother." Even in his own agony, as he fulfilled the very reason for which he came to this earth, to redeem mankind, Jesus showed us the infinite importance of our human relationships. This was also the culmination of joy in my own life, to see my own parents so blessed and filled with peace and joy and love, after all I had put them through in years past. God has not only restored all those "locust years," but He has given us the closest, most loving family relationship we could have ever dreamed! I don't believe it was *in spite of* all we went through, *but because of* all we went through!

If you look back over what seems to be those worst times of your life, they are the very things God has used to not only "grow you" but He will use you in those areas to help others going through similar circumstances! If you are in the MIDDLE of some of those worst circumstances right now, this is the secret of the true overcomer... to praise God and thank Him in the midst of those trials, whether you *feel* like it or not. When you want to chase away the enemy, when the walls are all crumbling around you, when you can't even see the tunnel – much less any light at the end – start the process you just learned all over again!

Be encouraged by those who have paved the way. Be encouraged that if one failure can be turned around, so can yours!

Remember your dream and goal and re-kindle that passion. Then do as Paul also admonishes:

"Keep your eyes on the prize."

If necessary, re-start your engine and do whatever it takes to get over the next hump. Don't grieve over lost time or territory, just keep going forward however slow and bumpy the process. There is a straight stretch ahead!

Don't see change and unexpected events as an enemy, but welcome them as new opportunities. Instead of asking God why this happened, ask Him what you are to do in the midst of it. Just wait and see how He will use you AND the circumstance for some greater good!

Begin to be glad when you see parts of your former life crumble. As God begins to sift out the wheat from the chaff, you will eventually be glad He removes the things you once held so tightly. I thank God I haven't always gotten what I prayed for, or I would be married to an abusive alcoholic who I truly thought I couldn't live without at age 18. Thank God he broke my heart!

Don't forget those "angels in disguise." God will send you mentors, buddies, coaches, supporters, family and friends, who will tell you the truth in love. These are your assigned encouragers, who care enough not to let you fall!

Never forget the importance of balance in all areas of your life and don't ever think you stand lest you fall! Just when you think you have reached the top and achieved all your goals, you just may have to be abased all over again. Remember "God resisteth the proud but exalts the humble." If you have never gotten to the end of yourself and been brought to your knees, it will happen! Scripture tells us that "Every knee shall bow, every tongue confess…" I thank God I was brought to the end of myself 30 years ago and most every day since. I know what I was and what I would be again, but for His amazing grace!

Keep realistic expectations! Many say, "If I don't expect much then I won't be disappointed." But I have found just the opposite. I am reminded that in this world we will have trials and tribulations, but He says, "I have overcome the world." If I were depending on my own power I would expect nothing. But I can do all things through Christ who strengthens me! When the process is slow, pray even more. When you have a setback and lose a little ground, gain more as you move forward again.

Remember the important things in life. They may not appear to be the most "urgent." But what will matter the most in the long run? The recent tragic attack on our nation made us all ask this question. The sowing and reaping process is proven and tried! The Dead Sea is stagnant because it doesn't flow onward. Let the Living Water flow through you-especially when you are thirsty yourself!

The last thing to remember is that you may forget all of this. But you can pick up and start again every time. I do it daily. The process I have found is fairly simple, but for me it has been profound:

PRAY !

I DON'T UNDERSTAND FULLY HOW PRAYER WORKS, OR WHY IT WOULD MAKE A DIFFERENCE TO THE CREATOR OF THE UNIVERSE WHAT I SAY! BUT, I HAVE LEARNED THE IMPORTANCE OF OBEDIENCE, AND GOD TELLS US TO PRAY WITHOUT CEASING!

My husband and I struggled through the first years of our married life without ever praying. But now we begin each morning in Bible study, daily devotionals and then prayer. Remember, this is the same couple that in our second year of marriage was screaming at one another in a drunken rage threatening divorce and destruction!

The P in PRAY stands for PRAISE.

I simply begin in PRAISE. I have learned that God inhabits our praises. I can worship Him no matter what I am going through or whatever my circumstances. I can't control myself at times much less those around me, so I simply thank God for who He is, for picking me up out of the gutter, and for allowing me to be used for his Glory!

The R stands for REPENT.

There is not a day that I live in a perfect way, so I always go to my Father in repentance. He has already forgiven my sins, for He paid the price on the cross two thousand years ago. But I go to Him in confession because I need cleansing. I need to remember things I said, thought or did each day that I shouldn't have done, and things I should have done that I didn't do.

The A stands for ASK.

He told us, "You have not because you ask not, and when you ask, you ask amiss." That means I have either not come boldly to Him and asked for His guidance or provision, or I have asked for things with selfish motives. So the A in PRAY I designate as *asking* for OTHERS first – not anything here for myself. As Christ always put others first, so must we. We are told to intercede and pray one for another, So I keep an ongoing prayer list of those who need prayer, whether they have asked me to pray for them or not. (I have a list of 5000 prayer requests from my radio program!) This would seem overwhelming if I didn't know how infinite God is – how His ways are so far above our ways.

The Y stands for YOURSELF.

This is what is usually put first – YOURSELF! By the time you have praised and thanked God for all He has done and brought you through and then repented before Him for all you did amiss or left undone; then by the time you go through all of the serious needs and prayer requests of those whose situations are far worse than yours, you will find you spend a lot less time focused on self. This is the most amazing thing for me! As one who spent the first 23 years of my life focusing every thought and action on poor pitiful ME, ME, ME, I thank God for bringing me to my knees. Some days I am flat on my face just thanking Him for delivering me from myself!

IT'S YOUR TURN NOW!

Now for an ATTITUDE OF GRATITUDE: So you don't forget, just start a list of the top ten things for which you are most thankful: Thank God for each one, while you jot it down! (This is your PRAISE)

Now take a minute to remind yourself of the counterfeit things that were, or are, still in your life that you sincerely KNOW God alone can remove: This is the REPENT part.

Next, if you didn't already do so, begin a prayer list. Begin with family and friends whom you know have special needs and add to it as other needs and requests come to you. Interceding to God on behalf of others is so powerful!

Lastly, we are to bring our prayers and petitions to him-everything! There is nothing too small, nothing too large for Him. We aren't responsible for His answers, just to trust Him. We will either get a yes, no or wait. But His answer and timing are always perfect!

Ten

PASS IT ON

If you didn't include this in the last section, who are the people in your past who have been your encouragers – those that if you had the opportunity, you would like to go back and just thank? It may be a family member, a teacher, a youth leader or Pastor; it may be a friend you haven't kept in touch with or even someone with whom things ended on a negative basis. For those where it is possible, could you send them a note or bless them with a surprise phone call? All I can say is that the one you may want to contact the least may turn out to be the greatest blessing! Remember the story of my high school teacher, Miss Alma? She was the one who had the audacity to put her arms around me and tell me that God had great plans for my life! I knew several years ago I had to go back and see her.

Back in 1988, I had lost 100 pounds, was happily married and had been teaching in St. Louis for 15 years when I was selected as Teacher of the Year. I was compelled to return to my hometown and thank the one who had so inspired me. Miss Alma, by then retired, was serving at a fish fry at her church social – fish and loaves of bread! How appropriate! As Jesus had fed the thousands so long ago, I envisioned the thousands Miss Alma had "fed" through the years; I knew that I was blessed to have been one of them.

As I approached her, I was immediately transported back

to that same insecure, anxious teenager, unable to speak. Once again I was enveloped in that warm, encouraging hug. "Oh Debbie! Look at you! You've lost a hundred pounds! And I heard you have become a teacher – I am so proud of you." I wanted to tell her what an inspiration she had been, how much I thanked her for not only saving my life, but also for inspiring me to be all that I had watched her model. I wanted to tell her how my life had changed and I had become a Christian and how I now share the same love and hugs with my students – as she had with me so many years before. But I was too choked up to say much of anything at the time. All I could mumble was, "Remember when I ran away from home and was suspended from school, and almost flunked out and…" But I couldn't even finish the sentence. "Why Debbie," Miss Alma whispered. "I only remember you as such a good student!" Miss Alma had seen the potential, not the problem. She saw me through the eyes of faith and loved me with the same unconditional love of Christ that my Mom and Dad also had. I didn't get to finish my thanks, at least not that day.

But I have kept in touch with Miss Alma and was invited last summer to speak at the graduation ceremony in her hometown. My parents who are now in their late seventies and travel all over the world to hear their "prodigal daughter" tell THEIR story, drove Miss Alma to the ceremony where I was speaking. As I had shared my past with thousands of my own students through the years, I shared with this graduating class how Miss Alma and my loving parents had literally saved my life when I wasn't even sure I wanted to be saved! I reminded them that God gives second, third and "hundredth" chances so that one day we will be the encourager to someone in need.

After the service, I saw a line of former students waiting to hug the beautiful 90 year old lady who had such an influence on so many. I watched parents of "troubled" kids flock to my parents for hope and encouragement to deal with their own children. There are some who won't know until eternity all the lives they have touched, but I have made sure that Miss Alma and my own parents certainly know! There is no doubt that one day soon they will hear our Savior say, "Well done, my good and faithful servant!"

As I have hosted a daily three-hour radio program for the past five years, called "Talk From the Heart, with Dr. Peppers," and a weekly television segment called "Shakin' the Salt," I have learned there are as many hurting and needy adults as there are children. I also know that God can still heal, restore marriages, and return prodigal sons and daughters. I am so grateful for all the faithful prayer warriors and seed-sowers in my life through the years-my parents, my husband, my family, former Sunday school teachers, my co-workers, my friends, my church family, and of course, Miss Alma.

Now that I have traveled throughout the United States as a member of the National Teachers Hall of Fame, speaking to thousands of schools, businesses and churches, I have always included the inspiring story of Miss Alma. As a radio and television talk show host, I have interviewed everyone from the President of the United States to prisoners on death row. But I never want to forget where I was thirty years ago and what I could have become, but for the grace of God. In all honesty, I should have been dead by now had I not gotten off that destructive path I was headed down. There are so many who are simply wandering around in the world that need to be reminded that "God has great plans for their life."

The process we have been through in this book isn't a magic formula, as I said before. But the principles are tried, tested and true because they follow what has been true for over 2000 years, and "The truth shall set you free."

IT'S YOUR TURN NOW! What you choose to believe, to act upon and to keep doing is up to you. You know your heart's desires, you know you CAN achieve those dreams with the power of God, and you know you can be set free from the negative thinking, the lies of the enemy and the old ties to the past. But remember this is a process, and a journey. You will still have trials and tribulations and new problems and issues you haven't even experienced. But this same process and these same tools and techniques can be applied and re-applied daily! Believe me I know!

For those of you who would like a few more strategies to get over those stumbling blocks as they come along, or to counter-attack the negativity, whatever the source, a few extension ideas will follow.

But first, according to Mark 11:24, we are to thank God *IN ADVANCE*, praying as if we have already received. The place that I am in my life right now, was at one time my "happily ever after." I knew I had submitted my life to God and was living in His will. Therefore, I made my desires and requests known to Him. But first and foremost I prayed that His will would be done. Any answer that followed was up to Him. If He was still working things out and gave me something else for the time-being, I thanked Him as painful as it might be. But I know that *All things work together for good to them that love God, and are called according to HIS purpose*. (Rom 8:28) When you get to this stage, you can write your final chapter. This is your "petition" to be made known to God in prayer and submission. Since He has already granted my "final chapter" requests, as you will see He will yours, be prepared to move even higher! You will find that the dream you had given up on was only the first stop on His glorious quest!

NOW IT'S YOUR TURN!

Just as I wrote the follow up to the Miss Alma story, what I have done with my teaching career and all I am doing now, YOU are going to write your final chapter. Be honest and bold in what you would like to see happen in your life, your family, your career, or whatever you choose. Remember, "You have not because you ask not and when you ask, you ask amiss!" So ask boldly, but seek His will and allow Him to examine your heart and motives!

YOUR FINAL CHAPTER

_____

_____

_____

_____

_____

_____

_____

_____

Continue Your Story on additional sheets as needed.

Extension Ideas:

*   *Keep an ongoing Journal of Your Progress*

*   *Begin and update a daily prayer list*

*   *Plan regular prayer time and Bible study*

*   *Join a Support Group in any needed areas*

*   *Find a good Church where the Word of God is preached – do not simply "follow tradition."*

*   *Begin a Healthy Eating, Exercise and Nutrition plan to fit your needs – one you will follow!*

*   *Send a "thank-you" note to past mentors whom you have never thanked!*

*   *Find an accountability partner, and be one as well!*

*   *Keep an ongoing self-evaluation checklist based on the lists you have completed. Be honest, but be patient in your growth. (Remember how long it took to get where you are.)*

FIND AND KEEP A LIST OF FAVORITE SCRIPTURES. HERE ARE A FEW OF MY FAVORITES – LOOK THEM UP AND USE THEM YOURSELF!

James 4:10   *1 John 1:9*

Phillipians 4:13   *Matthew 21:22*

Romans 12:2

Find ways to help others in areas where you have been healed.

Go back and re-read, remember, and do all of this as often as you can. It is like medicine to the soul.

I would never wish my "past life" on anyone. But I would pray that each of you would find the same joy, serenity and abundant life I have come to know! I am honored that I can be a living broken vessel to be used to help another on Life's Path. I pray that "my story" has encouraged you and will strengthen you on your quest. Remember,

"It's Your Turn Now!"

EXCITING NEW BOOK
ANSWERS AGE-OLD QUESTION

The author draws upon the Scriptural patterns and keys established by the Prophet Daniel to present readily understandable methods any believer can employ to *Tap into the Wisdom of God*. He shows from Scripture that it is both God's intention and will for man to turn to Him as the Source of knowledge.

You will learn seven major keys to receiving knowledge and find at least twenty-one practical encouragements to build your faith to seek God for answers.

Plus a Revelation
Discover for yourself the fascinating and prophetic secrets contained in Daniel Chapter Six, presented in the ninth chapter of this book. Chapter nine, which is actually a bonus book, presents an apparently undiscovered revelation showing more than one hundred parallels between Daniel and Jesus Christ.

"The most exciting thing I discovered was that what God did for Daniel, He can do for any believer!"
P.M., Bible Teacher, Kansas.

$10.95 + $1.75 Shipping

Impact Christian Books, Inc.
332 Leffingwell Ave., Suite 101,
Kirkwood, MO 63122

THE HEAVENS DECLARE . . .

William D. Banks

More than 250 pages!
More than 50 illustrations!

- Who named the stars and why?
- What were the original names of the stars?
- What is the secret message hidden in the stars?

The surprising, **secret message** contained in the earliest, original names of the stars, is revealed in this new book.

The deciphering of the star names provides a fresh revelation from the heart of **the intelligence** behind creation. Ten years of research includes material from the British Museum dating prior to 2700 B.C.

A clear explanation is given showing that early man had a sophisticated knowledge of One, True God!

$8.95 + $1.75 Shipping/Handling

ALIVE AGAIN!

William D. Banks

The author, healed over twenty years ago, relates his own story. His own testimony presents a miracle or really a series of miracles — as seen through the eyes of a doubting skeptic, who himself becomes the object of the greatest miracle, because he is Alive Again!

The way this family pursues and finds divine healing as well as a great spiritual blessing provides a story that will at once bless you, refresh you, restore your faith or challenge it! You will not be the same after you have read this true account of the healing gospel of Jesus Christ, and how He is working in the world today.

The healing message contained in this book needs to be heard by every cancer patient, every seriously ill person, and by every Christian hungering for the reality of God.

More than a powerful testimony — here is teaching which can introduce you or those whom you love to healing and to a new life in the Spirit! $4.95 + $1.75 Shipping/Handling

Impac Chris t ian Books

332 Leffingwell Ave., Suite 101
Kirkwood, MO 63122

AVAILABLE AT YOUR LOCAL BOOKSTORE, OR YOU MAY
ORDER DIRECTLY. Toll-Free, order-line only M/C, DISC,
or VISA 1-800-451-2708.

Visit our Website at *www. impactchristianbooks.com*

Write for *FREE* Catalog.